SIMPLY YOUTH MINISTRY

doug fields'
simply youth ministry
simplifying ministry...saving you time

RETURN TO:

SIMPLY YOUTH MINISTRY
1615 CASCADE AVE.
LOVELAND, CO 80538

17413858

PACK SLIP
SHIP TO: 1989917
Blake Lawyer
3150 Tates Creek Rd
Lexington,KY 40502
United States

BILL TO:
Blake Lawyer
3150 Tates Creek Rd
Lexington,KY 40502
United States

Page: 1 of 1
Order Date: 23-JUN-10
Order #:   3521779
Ord Ref: yhst-9597742652
Delivery ID: 17413858
Customer #:   1209896
Ordered By:
Ship Date: 23-JUN-10
Ship Method: Standard Delive
Cust Type: CONSUMER
Phone: 800-526-0404
Sales Rep: Group Publishin

PO #: Lawyer

PURCHASE ORDER #⬆

QTY.	✔	ITEM DESCRIPTION	PART #	RETAIL	FOR INTERNAL USE ONLY
1		SYM.MENTORING START TO FINISH.BK&CD-ROM	9780764463211		0

Items ordered but not included with this shipment   Expected Ship Date

** End of Pack Slip **

D1545223

THIS IS NOT AN INVOICE. DO NOT PAY FROM THIS DOCUMENT.
Thank You!

TOTAL CARTONS SHIPPED:

Simply Youth Ministry
1615 Cascade Ave.
Loveland, CO 80538

Visit our Web site: www.simplyyouthministry.com   See reverse for return policies and other information.

SIMPLY YOUTH MINISTRY

OUR COMMITMENT TO YOU...

Simply Youth Ministry is dedicated to providing you with quality tools and resources that save you time. But hey, sometimes you buy something that needs to be returned. No sweat—all we ask is that you read and follow our returns policy carefully, OK?

PROBLEMS WITH YOUR ORDER:

Give us a call at 1-866-9-simply and we'll be happy to help. The team at Simply Youth Ministry enjoys reading your feedback and comments. Seriously.

_____

_____

_____

_____

- ■ Enclose a copy of original invoice or pack slip
- ■ Affix this return shipping label
- ■ Pack & tape your package securely
- ■ Ship UPS or USPS—keep your shipping receipt.
- ■ Fill out "Reason for Return" area below

TO ENSURE PROPER CREDIT, PLEASE RETURN YOUR PACK SLIP OR INVOICE ALONG WITH YOUR SHIPMENT.

All returns should be shipped via UPS or USPS to **Simply Youth Ministry, 1615 Cascade Ave., Loveland, CO 80538.**

REASON FOR RETURN...

You can help us do an even better job with customer service. Take a second to let us know why you're returning this product. Go ahead and check all the reasons that apply. We won't take it personally.

____Already have product   ____Not what looking for   ____Ordered too many
____Arrived too late   ____Overstock   ____Will purchase later
____Defective/Damaged   ____Received wrong product   ____Did not order
____Too expensive

Are you requesting a refund check _____ or credit to your account_____

➡ # PRODUCT RETURNS POLICY

OUR RETURN POLICY IS SIMPLE

OK, we aren't really big fans of legal language, but some important people told us we need to make sure you read and understand our return policy. Here we go. You can return any item in saleable condition at any time, provided the products were purchased from Simply Youth Ministry by the customer to be credited. Customers are responsible for any and all shipping costs incurred to return the product to Simply Youth Ministry. To ensure proper credit, please return you packing slip or invoice along with each box shipped. If no packing or invoice information is given—items will be credited at the lowest price ever purchased from Simply Youth Ministry. If products are returned to Simply Youth Ministry, and a credit is not issued for any reason, the products will not be shipped back to the customer.

Ship via UPS or USPS to: **Simply Youth Ministry, 1615 Cascade Ave., Loveland, CO 80538.** Refunds can be issued upon request if your account has a credit balance. Please retain all shipping receipts and tracking numbers until return has been processed.

Got any questions about returns, or need help with other customer service issues? Give us a call at 1-866-9-simply!

We're always happy to hear back from customers. Got some ideas on how we can serve you better? Fire off an email to support@simplyyouthministry.com and let us know your thoughts! Thanks for making a difference in teenagers' lives!

Thanks so much for your help!

MENTORING
FROM START TO FINISH

HOW TO START AND MAINTAIN A HEALTHY
MENTORING PROGRAM FOR TEENAGERS

TAMI WRIGHT &
DR. GRANT T. BYRD
WITH DOUG FIELDS

Mentoring from Start to Finish
How to Start and Maintain a Healthy Mentoring Program for Teenagers

Credits
Authors: Tami Wright, Dr. Grant T. Byrd, and Doug Fields
Executive Developer: Nadim Najm
Chief Creative Officer: Joani Schultz
Assistant Editor: Rob Cunningham
Cover Art Director: Veronica Lucas
Designer: Veronica Lucas
Production Manager: DeAnne Lear

Unless otherwise indicated, all Scripture quotations are taken from the LIVE Holy Bible, New Living Translation, copyright © 1996, 2004, 2007. Used by permission of Tyndale House Publishers, Inc., Carol Stream, Illinois 60188. All rights reserved.

10 9 8 7 6 5 4 3 2 1   17 16 15 14 13 12 11 10
Printed in the United States of America.

TABLE OF CONTENTS

TABLE OF CONTENTS

PART TWO — PRACTICAL TOOLS AND RESOURCES

LETTER FROM TAMI & GRANT

Mentoring is BIG today but it isn't a new idea. The Bible is full of mentors and mentees! Jesus spent his time on earth mentoring a small group of guys to impact the world. You can multiply your ministry by unleashing men, women, and teenagers to mentor students one by one!

Starting a mentoring ministry isn't rocket science, but it sure can feel overwhelming to think about starting this effort to reach the youth in your church. That's why this resource was written—to give you start-to-finish practical help on running a ministry that might have more impact on your youth than any other event or program.

A one-on-one relationship with a caring and faith-filled adult can make a world of difference to a young person. Showing love, offering a listening ear, having fun, sharing real faith, and helping them see their purpose in life—these are but a few of the life-changing gifts mentors give their mentees.

We don't pretend to be experts at this, but we've learned enough through our years of working with mentoring programs to help others learn from successes AND failures. Keep in mind, your church size doesn't matter. In fact, we urge you to do a mentor program whether you have no youth ministry or a huge one. And here's some good news for youth pastors: You don't need to budget for this—other than funds for a few photocopies and some cookies and coffee for mentor meetings.

We hope you find this resource useful and effective. It was written for both youth pastors (like Grant) and church volunteers (like Tami)—anyone who has a heart for teenagers and loves God. Passionately search for adults in your congregation who can provide lasting and valuable friendships to your church's young people and your community's teenagers and who will at the same time reap more blessings than you can possibly imagine!

Tami Wright is the volunteer coordinator of Mentoring on Purpose at Saddleback Church, Lake Forest, California. She and her husband, Larry, have worked as volunteer youth ministry leaders over the years—Larry fitting right in with the students and Tami trying to provide some structure! They have two daughters, Amy married to Philip and Mandi married to Erin, and a grandson, Caleb. Tami is passionate about serving God, helping teenagers, and spending time with Caleb!

Dr. Grant T. Byrd is the Minister with Students at 1st Baptist Church of McKinney, Texas. He is the minister "with" not "to" or "of," because the students at the church serve alongside him! Grant has been in student ministry for more than 25 years. He has an incredibly beautiful wife (Jill) who has put up with him for 20 years, a teenage boy (Keegan) who keeps him honest, and a wonderful daughter (Darby) who wants to be a teenager TODAY! Grant is passionate about Jesus, his family, teenagers, and the Dallas Cowboys!

LETTER FROM DOUG

Dear youth ministry friend,

Thank you so much for caring so deeply about teenagers and knowing what's so vitally important and rewarding. I'm grateful for your leadership!

In my opinion, there are few things as rewarding within youth ministry as seeing teenagers become young adults who OWN their faith…just writing that gets me excited! I'm not sure many things in ministry can compare!

I think every youth worker wants to see teenagers maintain a vibrant relationship with God and be a committed follower of Jesus as they grow older. Unfortunately, this isn't happening in the large numbers that we'd like. I don't have all of the answers, but I do know one of the answers is to develop a team of caring adults who eagerly mentor and spend time with teenagers and firsthand demonstrate what it means to be a mature follower of Jesus.

So many teenagers lack strong role models in their lives, and even the most loving parents often feel overwhelmed as they strive to raise Christ-like kids in today's culture. The church has an opportunity—and an obligation—to focus its efforts on strengthening families. When a mentor comes alongside to offer support and encouragement not only does the teenager benefit, but so does the rest of the family. How's that for a win-win situation? In fact, throw in some more "wins" because of how the mentoring relationship helps the mentor and inspires growth and depth within the body of Christ!

That's just one of the reasons why I'm so excited about this resource from Tami Wright and Grant Byrd. They know what they're talking about! Years ago I asked Tami to develop a mentoring program that would surround our youth ministry. I desperately wanted it, but I didn't have the time to develop and lead it. Tami did and she did it as a volunteer. She's amazing! Also amazing is Dr. Grant Byrd! Don't let the Dr. fool you…he's a full-time youth worker who is just really smart—one of the nicest and respected youth workers I know who is serving kids, families, and the church in Dallas. Together, Tami and Grant will guide you as you consider the purpose of a mentoring program, how this kind of program can make a huge difference in your church and community, and what it takes to get things started. This is tremendously helpful material!

I'd encourage you to read this material with a team of leaders or parents. Find at least one other person with a similar passion for seeing teenagers become young adults who own their faith. This material is ready for your leadership to adapt it to your setting. If you've ever used any of Simply Youth Ministry's "Start to Finish" resources, you know that you'll find these pages stuffed with practical ideas based on years of experience with mentoring ministries. You'll be ready to go!

I'm praying that God will help your mentoring ministry impact the lives of countless teenagers and families in your community!

Blessings,

Doug Fields
Old Youth Pastor & Founder of Simply Youth Ministry

INTRODUCTION
MULTIPLYING YOUR IMPACT

A Quick Note

We—Tami and Grant—each bring unique experiences to the table—Tami coordinating a traditional adult-to-teenager program and Grant incorporating a peer-to-peer program. We've collaborated on this resource to offer you greater insight and wisdom on creating a healthy mentoring program for your youth ministry. In most cases, we've used "we" to talk about our ideas, suggestions, and stories. In a few instances, you'll see "I (Tami)" or a third-person reference. This simply highlights a unique experience or insight from our past.

We don't know your specific story. You might be a youth pastor or a volunteer or a parent. But we think we know a few things about you. You're passionate about seeing teenagers grow in their faith. You're committed to developing a quality youth ministry. You're excited about seeing young people discover God's purpose for their lives.

You're already a role model for your students. You have incredible influence on teenagers' lives. A mentoring program can expand and increase that influence!

If that's you, keep reading. If that's not you—well, keep reading anyway! God clearly has a plan for your life if this book has ended up in your hands! Mentoring offers you an opportunity to multiply the impact of your youth ministry by investing in mentors who will invest in the lives of teenagers in your church and community.

Mentoring is a valuable experience. In recent years, many books and websites have been devoted to the contribution of mentoring— mentoring in the workplace, mentoring between women, mentoring students at school, mentoring youth in the community.

There's a spiritual benefit from healthy mentoring, too: "A mentor can bring out the best in you and help you achieve God's unique mission for your life. They help you keep growing—in your roles, your goals, and your soul" (Rick Warren).

But is there a place within your youth ministry for mentoring? Why set up a mentoring program if you already have a vibrant youth program? Why bother if you have wonderful small groups for your teenagers?

How can you possibly add another activity to your already overworked youth ministry team? How can a mentoring ministry fit into the current structure?

Who can start this ministry? Who will support it? Who will serve as mentors, and how will you find the students who can benefit from a one-on-one relationship with a Christian adult in your church?

Why bother? We've found that whether you are a small rural church or a huge urban congregation, you have teenagers who don't feel comfortable in the mainstream youth group—for a wide range of reasons. But these young people still need the attention and nurture of a church community.

I (Tami) wasn't surprised by what I found as we launched a mentoring program within the Saddleback Church high school ministry. I had seen the same need in other churches, small and large. I found students disconnected from the mainstream youth program who needed a Christian adult to come alongside them and be their friend and encourager. I found students who needed some extra one-on-one interaction with a caring adult—even if those students already were involved in a small group. I found parents who were desperate for help in getting their teenagers involved in church. I found youth workers who cared deeply for their students and saw value in referring them to the mentoring program for additional support. I found that we could all work together to support these young people God had placed in our care.

In all churches, you find alienated youth. It can't be blamed solely on the youth ministry itself or the individual student. You find a thousand different reasons why students remain disconnected or distant. We can fill the gap with caring mentors for these students who otherwise would fall through that gap. And we can offer added value to those students who are already active in the mainstream youth group.

WHO will benefit?

Everyone benefits: students, their parents, the youth staff, the mentors, and the entire congregation.

WHO will launch and lead this program?

Well, it could be one of your current leaders or it could be someone else in your congregation who has a heart for teenagers, loves God, and can devote time to the program's growth and development. Your "ideal" person would probably have the gift of administration!

WHO will the mentors be?

They should be people from your church who have a heart for teenagers and a love for God. We've found that adults are usually the best mentors, but we also have seen mature teenagers become effective mentors to their peers and to younger students. You may find yourself drawn to a structure that includes this peer-to-peer dynamic, which can empower and release your teenagers to discover, develop, and use their spiritual gifts and abilities.

WHO will the students be?

Your answer will reflect your priorities as a church and youth ministry. In a large congregation, you might keep it limited to students who either attend your church or whose parents attend. You probably have teenagers who are falling through the cracks. But your focus may be on the teenagers in your surrounding community, or it may be a hybrid of students from your congregation and from your community. That's a decision for you and your church leadership to make.

TIP
How familiar are you with the spiritual gifts and talents of your current leaders? A youth ministry that multiplies its impact is a youth ministry with people serving where they're best gifted to serve.

TIP
Be wise. Don't chart the course for your mentoring program without input from your senior pastor and other key leaders in your congregation—unless you want to diminish your credibility and cripple the program before it's even out of the gates.

If you come across
other helpful resources
as you're developing
your mentoring ministry,
consider letting
us know at ideas@
simplyyouthministry.
com so we can pass
along the helpful
information to other
leaders!

This book will address many of the "how to" questions for creating a mentoring program. God will prove himself faithful as you go through some learning experiences in the first years of your program. There are always learning experiences, but the "first" experiences set the foundation for your program, and many of the ideas we share in this book come from our own experiences with various mentoring programs. Our prayer is that our successes and failures will provide a solid foundation for what God wants to accomplish in your own unique setting.

Many of the tools included here are adapted from different resources we've found useful over the years. *One Kid at a Time* from David C. Cook (no longer available) was one such resource. We've also found the following books to be valuable when we were setting up our mentoring programs:

- *Intensive Caring, Practical Ways to Mentor Youth* (Group Publishing)
- *Mentoring: How to Invest Your Life in Others* (Equip) by Tim Elmore
- *New Directions for Youth Ministry* (Group Publishing) by Wayne Rice, Chap Clark, and others

WHAT IS MENTORING?
MULTIPLYING YOUR IMPACT

Picture yourself sitting in a Starbucks—this probably isn't too difficult. While there, you're watching a veteran worker train a new employee. The veteran is serving as the model for the rookie, drawing on her experience and knowledge to help prepare this worker as he begins his new job. She's been in his shoes, of course, so she's able to speak wisely about the challenges he'll face in his first day, his first week, and his first month on the job. In a very real sense, the veteran employee is a mentor.

There are many ways to define what a mentor is. The dictionary defines a mentor as someone who serves as a trusted counselor or teacher to another person. The word "mentor" comes from Homer's epic poem *The Odyssey*. In fact, it was a person's name. The man, "Mentor," was entrusted with the education and well-being of Telemachus, son of Mentor's friend, King Odysseus. When the king left to fight in the Trojan War, he put his beloved son into the care of his faithful friend.

What is a mentor in our 21st century context?

A mentor is like a loving older brother or sister who wants what's best for younger brothers or sisters, looking for ways to help them grow into full spiritual maturity and helping them reach their full leadership potential.

A mentor is someone who offers strengths, resources, and networks (friendships/contacts) to help a mentee reach goals.

A mentor is someone who enters a voluntary relationship of trust and mutual respect with another person, in which learning happens as a byproduct. Developing a healthy friendship is more important than teaching specific principles or ideas. Put another way, mentoring has more to do with who you are than what you do.

That means a mentoring program is not a one-size-fits-all concept. The structure that best fits your church and your youth ministry may

TIP
Take a few minutes to think about the people who've helped shape you. What individuals have served as mentors? How are you different today because of the role they've played in your life?

A quick note: You will see some sidebars titled Peer-to-Peer Tip. These tips are geared to those of you who want to run a teenager-to-teenager mentoring program.

PEER-TO-PEER TIP
Many teenagers will grasp these truths, although some may need some help and guidance along the way. The trust and respect dynamic will be different between two teenagers compared to an adult mentor and a teenage mentee.

TIP

It's important to be open to "accidental" opportunities to invest in the life of a teenager, too!

not be appropriate for another congregation on the other side of town. Our goal in this book is not to offer a prescriptive list of ways this program must be implemented. We simply draw on our own experiences to share some insights and principles that can help you create a mentoring program that multiplies the impact of your youth ministry.

For our purposes, mentoring is intentionally investing time to help a teenager pursue God's purposes and plans for life. Mentoring is not about a specific set of questions and answers. Mentoring is allowing a person to learn from you. You'll start getting into the habit of challenging teenagers to reach new heights in life. Affirming students in what they are accomplishing now will spur them on! Praying with teenagers through the good and bad times will help them understand what it really means to have a relationship with God. Talking through specific Scriptures will encourage teenagers to go to the Bible to find the answers they need.

BIBLICAL FOUNDATION
MULTIPLYING YOUR IMPACT

The God of all creation began the world with a desire to interact with humanity (Genesis 1:27). This plan hasn't changed. God desires to be in fellowship with us (Romans 8:38-39). He seeks us out (2 Chronicles 16:9). He's a loving God who desires personal interaction (John 3:16).

You also can find that desire for personal interaction in every man and woman—and every teenager. We all desire to interact with others and develop relationships. No one wants to be seen as "just another person." Everyone has a need to be seen as an individual—and this need came from our Creator (Psalm 139). God sees everyone individually and seeks a personal relationship with each of us (2 Peter 3:9). It is a relationship that can be strengthened and deepened, and mentoring can play a part in that growth process for the teenagers in your ministry.

God was the first mentor—even though that word wasn't used to describe the original divine interaction with humanity. God mentored Adam in the garden about which trees should be avoided and which trees were acceptable. *"You may freely eat the fruit of every tree in the garden—except the tree of the knowledge of good and evil. If you eat its fruit, you are sure to die" (Genesis 2:16-17).*

MENTORS IN THE BIBLE
MULTIPLYING YOUR IMPACT

Each of us needs healthy relationships. This is God's design. Fortunately, we can find mentoring relationships throughout the Bible to serve as models and guides. We've identified a handful of these relationships; in each case, we see the rewards of a mentor's investment in another person's life.

Jesus and His Disciples

It's quite likely you've never thought of Jesus as a mentor, but in many ways, that's who he was to his disciples. Jesus taught by example and embodied the principles of healthy mentoring. He spent considerable time with the multitudes, but the Gospels reveal that he made it a priority to prepare his 12 disciples for ministry.

Jesus challenged his disciples to grow, just like a mentor should. He spent time with his disciples in a wide variety of settings, just like a mentor should. He developed a friendship with his disciples yet he was much more than just a friend—the same is true of an effective mentor.

And he prayed for his disciples, a habit that a healthy mentor also should develop. Closely read these words from John:

[20]*"I am praying not only for these disciples but also for all who will ever believe in me through their message.* [21]*I pray that they will all be one, just as you and I are one—as you are in me, Father, and I am in you. And may they be in us so that the world will believe you sent me.*

[22]*"I have given them the glory you gave me, so they may be one as we are one.* [23]*I am in them and you are in me. May they experience such perfect unity that the world will know that you sent me and that you love them as much as you love me.* [24]*Father, I want these whom you have given me to be with me where I am. Then they can see all the glory you gave me because you loved me even before the world began!" (John 17:20-24).*

Jesus understood the principle of spiritual multiplication. He knew that this ragtag group of men could impact their world, so he invested in them and poured his life into seeing them fulfill God's plan for their lives. That plan became even more potent through the work of the Holy Spirit (Acts 1:8).

In his book *The Greatest Mentors in the Bible*, author Tim Elmore highlights 12 factors that Jesus included in his mentoring ministry. These are important to consider when creating a biblically based mentoring program:

1. Initiative (Luke 6:12-13)
2. Proximity (Mark 3:14)
3. Friendship (John 15:15)
4. Example (John 13:15)
5. Commitment (John 13:1)
6. Responsibility (Mark 6:7)
7. Knowledge (Luke 8:9-10)
8. Trust (Matthew 10:1-8)
9. Evaluation (Luke 10:17-20)
10. Goal (Matthew 4:19)
11. Power (John 20:22)
12. Launch (Matthew 28:19-20)

Jesus displayed these characteristics when working with his disciples and then commanded them to mentor and lead others, using the same techniques. Jesus began his public ministry by recruiting the 12 disciples. He spent most of his remaining ministry time training them. They saw the importance of mentoring through Jesus' life.

And Jesus' final words in the Great Commission (Matthew 28:19-20) include the command to go make more disciples—in our

TIP
Each one of these traits can be a great idea for a training session with your team of mentors.

PEER-TO-PEER TIP
Encourage your teenagers to see their school campuses as part of this "mission field" and talk with them about the implications for their lives.

neighborhood, in our region, in other nations. This mentoring process—another way to think of the word "discipleship"—was the way that the kingdom of God would be expanded and fulfilled.

Moses to Joshua (Exodus 24:13)

Moses set an example for Joshua through his intimacy with God. Consider this verse from the Old Testament: *Inside the Tent of Meeting, the Lord would speak to Moses face to face, as one speaks to a friend. Afterward Moses would return to the camp, but the young man who assisted him, Joshua son of Nun, would remain behind in the Tent of Meeting (Exodus 33:11).* Joshua saw the depth of Moses' relationship with God, and he wanted to experience the same thing in his life.

We also can see that Moses impacted Joshua's life because he had faith in this young man. He included Joshua on the team that spied out the Promised Land. This is similar to how a mentor will demonstrate trust and confidence in a young mentee. Like Moses, the mentor must put faith in the mentee.

Naomi to Ruth (Ruth 1:6-18)

The most prominent examples of biblical mentoring involve an older mentor and younger mentee. Can you think of any instances where the roles were reversed?

Naomi was an example and friend to her daughter-in-law Ruth. Ruth had a husband named Mahlon (Ruth 4:10) who died, but Naomi helped fill a void. She mentored Ruth with availability and empathy. Naomi insisted that Ruth return home to her native land, but Ruth had become attached to the guidance and love of her mother-in-law.

Ruth's response was remarkable: *16"Don't ask me to leave you and turn back. Wherever you go, I will go; wherever you live, I will live. Your people will be my people, and your God will be my God. 17Wherever you die, I will die, and there I will be buried. May the Lord punish me severely if I allow anything but death to separate us!" (Ruth 1:16-17).* Ruth needed godly counsel and empathy, and she received it from Naomi.

Eli to Samuel (1 Samuel 3:1)

The best news we can find in the mentor relationship between Eli the priest and Samuel the apprentice is that God uses imperfect mentors. Eli was father to two sons who were evil and wicked. God told Eli what would happen to his two sons. *"And to prove that what I have said will come true, I will cause your two sons, Hophni and Phinehas, to die on the same day!" (1 Samuel 2:34).*

Samuel was teachable, an important trait in a mentee. Eli's own sons didn't learn from their father, but the priest found that Samuel had a teachable attitude. Eli could see that God had a distinct purpose for Samuel. In 1 Samuel 3, Eli challenged Samuel to discover his purpose directly from God.

Elijah to Elisha (1 Kings 19:16)

Elijah took Elisha under his wing and taught him everything he knew (1 Kings 19:21). Elisha started out following Elijah as a teenager (1 Kings 19:16). Elisha stayed with Elijah and would not leave his mentor (2 King 2:1-15).

Elijah encouraged Elisha to stay home while he went to Bethel but Elisha did not (2 Kings 2:4). Elijah was a great prophet but God used Elisha to perform even greater miracles. Mentors can instruct and guide their mentees and help them grow spiritually.

Paul to Timothy (Acts 16:3)

This is one of most well-known mentoring relationships in the Bible, and it's a great source of inspiration for older mentors investing in young people. You might encourage your mentors to read 1 Timothy and 2 Timothy for insights and wisdom. Paul's message to Timothy can be summarized with these words: *[11] Teach these things and insist that everyone learn them. [12] Don't let anyone think less of you because you are young. Be an example to all believers in what you say, in the way you live, in your love, your faith, and your purity (1 Timothy 4:11-12).*

Read 1 Samuel 3:7. This statement about Samuel is true for many teenagers in your youth ministry, too!

PEER-TO-PEER TIP
A willingness to learn is an especially important trait for teenage mentors. They're investing in younger students' lives, but they still need investment from older leaders and coaches—and they need to be teachable.

PEER-TO-PEER TIP
As you work with teenage mentors, 1 Timothy 4:12 will become an increasingly meaningful verse. Encourage these mentors to become an example to others through actions, attitudes, and choices.

TIP

Want some more examples from the life of Paul? Check out Barnabas to Saul/Paul (Acts 11:25-26); Paul to Silas (Acts 15:22); and Paul to Onesimus (Philemon 1:10).

Paul understood how to impact a person's life through mentoring—even though he didn't use that word—because he had been given a great example in Barnabas (Acts 11:25). Paul challenged Timothy to be all that God designed him to be. Timothy learned the concept of mentoring and then passed this example on to others.

ONE FAMILY'S STORY
MULTIPLYING YOUR IMPACT

If you wonder about the effectiveness and impact of a mentoring program, you may find inspiration in Sarah's story. She's a single mom whose family has been strengthened by mentors investing in the lives of her two daughters. And not surprisingly, she also benefited from mentors when she was younger.

"My first encounter with a mentor was when I was in the seventh grade," she recalls. "A girlfriend and I were chosen to spend a day with two college students at their home. I never forgot that experience because being raised in the 'barrio' (Hispanic neighborhood), I was able to see that there was more outside the neighborhood that I lived in."

When Sarah was in her 20s, she experienced another mentoring relationship that ultimately sowed the seed for her to become a Christian. She worked with a woman who became an example of what it meant to follow Christ—the first time Sarah had encountered someone who "talked about God as a real person." That woman's influence continues to this day in Sarah's life.

"I was extremely shy, and she pushed me gently to do things that I was too afraid to do before I met her," Sarah says. "I will never forget her because I am who I am today thanks to her gentle and loving influence."

Because of those experiences, Sarah immediately responded when her church launched a mentoring program. She wanted her daughters to benefit from mentors in their lives, too. She knew that her girls would find their mentors to be women they could talk to openly—even about issues or topics they might not want to discuss with mom.

Her daughter Angie had a rough start to her teenage years, battling depression along the way. But she opened up to her mentor, Jane, and the two developed a deep, trusting relationship. Jane became

TIP
Sometimes you'll see an immediate impact from a mentor's involvement, and sometimes you won't see it for a long time. But remember: A mentor's goal is to have a lasting, eternal impact on a teenager's life.

TIP
Encourage your
mentors to write down
a teenager's important
calendar days—
birthdays, vacations,
holidays, any major
losses of loved ones,
start of the new school
year, and so on.

a vital part of the support network that carried Angie through that difficult season of life.

"Jane is a very important person in Angie's life," Sarah says. "When my daughter's tonsils were taken out, Jane was there. Jane never forgets my daughter's birthday and always calls her to see how she is doing. I don't know how many years they've known each other now, but I do know that Jane will always be part of my daughter's life one way or another. I have thanked Jane personally because in today's society there aren't too many people who take time out of their busy lives to reach an adolescent."

Sarah had similar praise for the relationship between her other daughter, Vanessa, and her mentor, Kari.

"Kari was godsent for Vanessa," Sarah remembers. "From the very beginning God chose the perfect mentor for Vanessa. Vanessa always looked forward to meeting with Kari. Again, when Vanessa was having a problem or wanted to talk to someone about it, she called Kari. She always came home in a good mood after spending time with Kari. One day Vanessa came home and said to me that she did not know what she would do without Kari in her life."

These mentoring relationships provided Sarah with peace and joy as she watched godly women invest in the lives of her daughters.

"Being an adolescent is a very difficult part of growing up, and having a godly and loving mentor makes life a little easier," Sarah says.

MENTOR TESTIMONIES
MULTIPLYING YOUR IMPACT

"My entire experience with Katie has been extremely rewarding and valuable to both Katie and me."

"What I put into being a mentor was more than returned to me in blessings. I still feel like I was the one being mentored and have gained a whole other family in my life as a result."

"Though progress seemed slow at times, I witnessed God's work in my student by the end of our year commitment. I learned much about God's humor and grace through our relationship, which took me out of my comfort zone and stretched me. That experience in turn gave me confidence to do more for God, knowing it was him working when I showed up."

"I was told by Brandon's family that I played a huge part during a critical period in Brandon's high school 'growing up' years—as if he would have gone down the wrong path had I not intervened. I deflect this and offer that Brandon had it in him all along; he just needed a friend—outside the family—to listen to him and be a buddy."

"My involvement with Karl has had a really positive impact on my family, mainly with my kids (10 and 12) because they get to see me in a servant's role in a voluntary capacity. They recognize the difference in being forced to serve and wanting to serve. It puts me on higher ground in their eyes and allows me to hold them to a higher standard as well."

TIP

Consider changing or omitting the names of students when using promotional quotes or statements. It's a simple but smart step that can ensure and enhance the trust element of your mentoring ministry. Similarly, changing or omitting the mentors' names from these statements can be a wise decision.

PEER-TO-PEER TIP

Compile your own list of comments from teenage mentors to use in future promotions and updates on your mentoring ministry's impact.

STUDENT TESTIMONIES
MULTIPLYING YOUR IMPACT

TIP

After your first round of mentoring, make sure you get testimonies from teenagers. Sometimes we remember to get feedback from the mentors but overlook the teenagers.

"Having Dan in my life has been a godsend. Dan and I are great friends, and my life would have been radically different without Dan in my life. I would have been hard pressed to find a guy that I could talk to, to come and seek advice for issues with my mother, school, or even more secret personal struggles. Dan has helped me even with teaching me how to be polite and eat correctly in a restaurant. Dan has been a father figure for me, and since my own father is non-Christian, and since I do not live with my father—being that my parents are divorced—this has become something extremely important to me. I'm exceedingly glad to have Dan in my life, and I hope that we will continue on with our relationship well past high school."

"For me the mentoring program was one of the greatest experiences of my exchange year. When I returned to my country, I missed the conversations between Anna and me a lot. Also, it makes church more personal and builds bridges between different generations in church."

"I was originally a mentee when I was in eighth grade. My mentor met with me weekly and talked about life. He treated me like a grown-up, and I had such a positive experience that I became a mentor my junior year. I discovered that being a mentor is an even better experience than being mentored!"

DEFINING YOUR PURPOSE
CREATING THE PROGRAM

Why are you creating a mentoring program? This is a foundational question that must be answered before the first mentors and students are recruited. We believe a general reason is to create opportunities for students to grow personally and spiritually through involvement and support from caring mentors. This happens as the mentor and student spend time together in conversation and shared activities.

As you're answering that question—why are we creating this program?—seek God's guidance. Ask him to direct your program and to be a vital part of every aspect. God is interested in every detail, every decision, and every mentor and student match. God wants to give you wisdom as you plan and develop the program. Expect him to do the work as you make yourself available. You may have an idea of how you see this new ministry in your church, but be open to God's leading. He may have something totally different in mind.

From the very beginning, find someone to pray for you and the program as it develops. Perhaps that person can become a prayer coordinator to organize prayer partners who will pray for the mentors, students, and the ministry as it grows. Have you picked up on our belief that prayer is vital to your program's success?

We also believe in the benefits of a purpose statement that clearly explains why your program exists and what you hope God accomplishes through it. Create a purpose statement for your mentoring program that complements your youth ministry's purpose statement, if it has one—it might be called a mission statement or vision statement or some similar phrase.

For example, the Saddleback high school ministry purpose statement goes like this:

*"Our youth ministry exists to **REACH** non-believing students, to **CONNECT** them with other Christians, to help them **GROW** in their faith, and to challenge the growing to **DISCOVER** their ministry and **HONOR** God with their lives."*

PEER-TO-PEER TIP
If you adopt or include the peer-to-peer dynamic, be prepared to explain why. Some parents may have reservations or concerns, and some leaders in your congregation may question what impact one teenager can have on the life of another young person. Answer these questions in advance, and be ready to explain—not debate or argue, but explain.

TIP
One of the greatest challenges in any ministry is finding balance between making plans and remaining flexible. God will give you ideas and inspiration, but he also may throw a curveball or two your way!

And here is the purpose statement we used for the mentoring program:

*"Our mentoring program exists to support and challenge students, on a one-to-one basis and over time, to **GROW** in maturity and in their faith, to help them **DISCOVER** God's purpose and ministry for their lives, bringing **HONOR** to God."*

Don't work alone on your purpose statement. Get others involved: youth ministry leaders, volunteers, parents, students, pastors, teachers, random strangers—OK, we're just kidding about the strangers. But your vision and purpose will be stronger with diverse input.

Once you've created your purpose statement, add guidelines to your purpose statement so that the church leadership, parents, potential mentors, and students can see your vision and know that you have thought this all out and are ready to go with it.

Here are guidelines you might include (as found in the Purpose Statement and Guidelines, on p. 79), or you can come up with your own as God leads:

- Mentors will "be there" for students—caring for them, guiding them, being a role model, and encouraging them.

- Students who request mentoring or come to us as a result of parents' requests or youth ministry leadership referrals will be brought to the attention of the mentoring coordinator(s). Students will be paired with mentors with an attempt to match interests, life experience, geographical location, and so on.

- When a church member indicates a desire to serve as a mentor, he or she will be asked to fill out an application. The application will be used to screen the mentor and identify his or her interests and abilities that would be useful for matching the applicant with a student. After the required interview and reference and background checks are complete, the mentor will go through an initial training and then be matched with a student. Mentors will be asked to make a commitment of at least one year to the program.

- Mentors will need the approval and support of parents, and cannot and should not take the place of parents. The mentor coordinator will meet initially with the parent(s), mentor, and student to explain the purpose of the mentoring relationship, obtain the permission of the parent(s), and schedule a first meeting for the student and mentor. A parent will be required to sign a Parent Affirmation form, giving permission for the relationship and providing emergency information and other important data.

- The mentor and student will discuss the required commitments, decide on a regular time to meet, and set some goals they can accomplish together. A Mentoring Covenant can be signed between mentor and student, indicating their commitment.

- Mentors are expected to attend the youth ministry volunteer staff meetings for ongoing support where they can voice their concerns and receive encouragement and prayer from each other. Also, additional training can be provided for mentors during the meetings.

- The coordinator will have a team to assist with the various responsibilities of the mentor program.

PEER-TO-PEER TIP
When a teenager applies to be a mentor, require parental involvement in the interview and parental approval of the young person's service as a mentor. Remember, you're working with a minor—even when the minor is serving as a role model with younger students.

TIP
If you don't already have meetings for training, supporting, and challenging your volunteer leaders, here's a great opportunity to start!

- The mentoring coordinator and team will be available to advise, inform, and encourage the mentors. They will also be available to the parents of the mentored teenagers if the need arises.

After creating your guidelines, meet with the youth ministry staff and other church leaders to give them your vision and answer their questions. You may want or need to meet with the senior pastor or church elders, depending on the structure and "personality" of your congregation. Don't stress. These upfront meetings can help you build a stronger foundation and produce better results down the road.

The Christian Association of Youth Mentoring (www.caym.org) has a great resource manual entitled "Starting a Mentoring Ministry," which includes a chapter on getting your church on board. This resource provides answers to such questions as, "Do we need this type of ministry," "Does it work?" "Is mentoring safe?" "Do we have enough people for this ministry?" "What about insurance?" and "How much will it cost?"

By the way—don't let cost scare you. You may be able to run the program without a budget if the youth ministry picks up the cost of the fingerprinting and background checks. Plus, most prospective mentors are willing to pay that cost themselves. The other expenses should be minimal, such as refreshments for meetings and the cost of reproducing materials.

TIP

If God is leading you to launch this ministry, he'll find a way to provide you with all the resources you need. Remember: He's God.

A mentoring program should uniquely reflect its youth ministry and congregation. We don't believe in a cookie-cutter approach to ministry, so we've done our best to fill this book with recommendations and transferable principles. If you attempt to imitate or copy another program, you'll almost assuredly run into problems. Seek God's direction as you create and implement your program; God knows you, your church, and your community even better than you do!

Program Length
Consider creating a year-long program that begins in either January (the new calendar) or September (the new school year). This length will give your mentors and students plenty of time to develop healthy, meaningful relationships. It also gives mentors a chance to experience an entire cycle of seasons with the student—particularly beneficial if the teenager is involved in a wide range of activities or sports.

Can a shorter program work? Certainly. You may choose to structure a shorter program more tightly. You also might want to offer curriculum for the mentor to use each week; Grant's experiences include a six- to 10-week program that used this approach. (You can find the curriculum he used on p. 83.)

Program Scope
If your junior high and high school students are integrated or if your two ministries work together closely, you may want to offer the mentoring program to all teenagers. But each age bracket does present unique challenges and opportunities. A mentor who is successful with junior high students might not be the right fit for high school students, and vice versa. Any youth ministry will benefit from mentors who feel a specific call to either younger or older teenagers.

Program Coordinator
Most youth pastors won't have the time to become the coordinator of a mentoring program, unless they're surrounded by a solid

TIP
A program that follows a calendar year or a school year may not be best for your ministry. You may decide that it's better to set a time commitment after the right mentor match is made.

PEER-TO-PEER TIP
Using curriculum or providing greater structure can improve the peer-to-peer experience for both the mentor and the younger student.

TIP
We're big fans of providing unique environments for junior high students and high school students. Mentoring is a one-on-one experience, of course, but you might suggest a different mix of activities for mentors working with younger teenagers or find other ways to specifically target and minister to your students. Your mentors also will face different challenges.

team of other leaders—paid, volunteer, or both. In most cases, the mentoring program coordinator will either be a current leader willing to step into a new role or a new leader from within your congregation. It's important that the leader of this new ministry have a passion for what you're trying to accomplish—and if you're that person, THANKS for investing in students' lives!

If you're still searching for the right person to lead the program, don't give up. God will lead you to that individual—maybe not as quickly as you'd like, but trust him. Pray that God would lead you to someone who has a passion for teenagers and who is not afraid to take a risk. You want someone who will rely on the Holy Spirit for guidance. Ideally, this person will have the gift of administration or at least be detail-oriented.

This candidate does not need any other special gifts, talents, or credentials, such as a marriage and family therapist license. Your team will probably benefit from the assistance of a professional counselor, but it isn't essential for the coordinator to be this person. The coordinator just needs to be willing to accept support and be discerning to know how God is leading.

Maybe you, the reader, are considering starting this program and want to approach your church's high school ministry with this idea.

Here's what we know: If God is creating the desire to launch a mentoring program—or any other new ministry in your church—then he will provide the right person or team to lead it. Recruit a team of parents, students, and other leaders to pray daily until God opens the right door, and then ask this team to continue praying for the effectiveness and impact of the program once it begins.

Leadership Team

Whether the coordinator is a staff member or a volunteer, the stability and success of the ministry, as well as its sustainability, will depend on eventually having a strong team. What members are needed for this leadership team? That depends on the size of the ministry, of course, but at a bare minimum you could have—besides the coordinator or team leader—a prayer coordinator, a trainer, an interviewer/match maker, and one mentor coach for the men and one for the women. One person could fill more than one position, provided they have the time and capacity to do so. (The resource manual from the Christian Association of Youth Mentoring has good information on building a team.)

Look at the current mentors who are reliable and return your calls and who might have the gifts of encouragement, teaching, or discernment. Pray about them becoming a part of the team and then ask them as God leads. The coordinator should meet regularly with members of this leadership team, perhaps before the regular meetings with the mentors, or over dinner or coffee occasionally.

Gender Balance
Your program will benefit from having a person that can help the coordinator recruit and train mentors of the opposite sex. In other words, if your coordinator is female, it would be good to have a male leader who can interview potential guy mentors and meet with potential guy mentees, and then meet with both of them for the initial introduction meeting.

Paul was the man for the job in Tami's program. He was great at meeting with guy students to explain what this mentoring stuff was all about. He had a wonderful way of talking with students and encouraging them. This may not surprise you, but in many cases, it's tougher to get started mentoring a young man. Girls are often much easier to talk with and may share their deepest feelings within one meeting, while a guy may take six months to open up!

Crisis Counselor
This can be a friend at church who has experience with counseling youth and families. God blessed me (Tami) with Tracy, a talented gal who was already working as a volunteer in the high school

TIP
Having these team members in place is certainly an ideal situation. However, depending on the number of volunteers on your team, one person may have to carry a lot of this load. It's a heavy load to carry, so it's important that you have the right person in place.

PEER-TO-PEER TIP
Your teenage mentors
will require coaching—
and their needs will be
different from the needs
of an adult mentor.
Consider training
coaches who will
specialize in working
with your teenage
mentors.

ministry. She's a former licensed family and marriage therapist, so when a mentor or student had a problem, I could consult with her for advice. If the coordinator is on the church staff, he or she will have access to therapists or pastors who can advise them. Of course, matters of a serious nature should be brought before the youth ministry leaders or appropriate pastor on the church staff.

Mentor Coaches

Once your program has grown and you have a good number of mentor and student matches, it may become difficult for the coordinator to effectively communicate with all of the mentors. At that point, he or she should pray about which mentors would make good coaches. They need to be reliable and good communicators. They will shepherd mentors under them and report to the coordinator. The coaches should speak or communicate by email monthly with their designated mentor team members, collecting the Monthly Mentor Reports (see p. 136) and reporting to the coordinator.

ANSWERING PARENTS' QUESTIONS
CREATING THE PROGRAM

Every program and church is unique, so you may encounter questions that we haven't seen in other mentoring programs. Here are our thoughts on some of the most common questions we've heard from parents over the years.

What is the goal of the mentoring program?
The primary goal is for the student to grow personally and spiritually through involvement with and support from a caring mentor. This happens as the mentor and student spend time together in conversation and shared activities.

What do you expect of me/us as parent(s)?
The mentoring program won't require a major time commitment from families. But it is important for parents to support the student's involvement and the program's primary goal. (If you and your leadership team create any kind of quarterly meeting for parents, make sure you inform families about this opportunity.)

How much time is involved for my child?
The typical commitment is between 60 and 90 minutes each week. Some weeks might be a longer commitment, depending on the planned activity for the mentor and the student.

What is the cost for the program?
There is no major cost for families. We encourage families to give their students some extra cash for bigger, more expensive activities; mentors shouldn't be asked to bear the entire cost of the mentoring relationship.

Is this safe for my child?
Each mentor will go through a background check with our congregation because we value the safety and well-being of all children and young people associated with our church. (If a family is extremely concerned, then it might be a challenging fit for the program. One possible solution would be asking the mentor to meet with the student at the family's home.)

PEER-TO-PEER TIP
Some of these questions and answers will work well for the peer-to-peer program, but others will need to be revised based on how you're building your program.

TIP
You'll get a wide range of responses from parents—as you probably do for any aspect of your youth ministry! Some will be supportive, some will be reluctant, and some will just be ambivalent. Providing lots of information at the beginning will help address most parental concerns and questions.

Where will these mentoring times take place?
We leave this up to the family, the student, and the mentor. The mentor and student can meet at a local fast food restaurant or a coffee house—or the family's home. If they have a common interest, that could open the door to a natural meeting place. We encourage mentors and families to be flexible on this topic as you work together.

When will they meet?
This is highly flexible and depends on a variety of factors including the student's other commitments, the mentor's work schedule, common interests, and family commitments. It can happen before school, after school, in the evenings, or on the weekends. This is something that can be worked out between family and mentor when you first meet.

Will the mentor be driving my child?
The mentor can come to your house to pick up your student, or you could transport your teenager to the meeting location. (If the student is older, he or she may already have a driver's license and vehicle.)

What happens if things don't work out well for my student?
Most students and mentors have positive experiences in mentoring programs. If any problem does arise, we will be available to help resolve the conflict. If the match isn't right, we're willing to find a different mentor for your student.

PEER-TO-PEER OPTIONS
CREATING THE PROGRAM

In general, we've found the greatest success matching adult mentors with teenage students. But you may have a limited pool of adult mentors, or perhaps you have some high school juniors or seniors who are particularly mature. You might want to include a peer-to-peer component in your program. I (Grant) have been involved in such programs, and I've seen tremendous fruit in the lives of both mentors and mentees.

You should still use an application and interview process for teenage mentors, and you'll probably be more focused on the maturity level of the applicant. Has this student been faithful in other ministries? Can this student be trusted? Does this student have spiritual depth and maturity essential to a mentoring relationship?

A 17-year-old may not be an effective mentor to a 16-year-old, but this person might be a good fit with a seventh- or eighth-grade student. We recommend an age gap of at least three years if you include the peer-to-peer option. This will let the mentee benefit from someone who has a little more maturity.

Teenage mentors usually will require more oversight than their adult counterparts. We suggest meeting with teenage mentors each week to discuss their mentoring relationship. I (Grant) have used curriculum in peer-to-peer programs (see p. 83 in Part Two of this resource), and if you make a similar choice, the weekly meeting is a good place for the coordinator or coach to review the curriculum with the teenage mentors.

We don't recommend that you *only* use teenagers as mentors in your program, but it might be an option to consider. Just remember that it will probably require more hands-on involvement from your leaders and coaches, and that it won't be the right fit for all students.

PEER-TO-PEER TIP
Consider revising the application and other documents found in Part Two to reflect the unique needs of a peer-to-peer option.

PEER-TO-PEER TIP
If you use a peer-to-peer option, consider some tighter restrictions on where the mentor and mentee meet. In general, a 17-year-old probably shouldn't be given as many freedoms in this area as an adult mentor.

Every church is different. Some churches have a "staff" of one volunteer youth pastor who also works a 9-to-5 job to pay the bills. Some youth ministries have a paid staff of 10 people. You probably fall somewhere in between.

The youth ministry team will probably welcome some extra help in caring for students. As you create and launch the mentoring program, it's important that it not be viewed as competition. Instead, this is another way to help your church and your youth group minister to students.

Many of your volunteers already are having conversations that will help identify students who can benefit by having a mentor. Volunteers and paid staff also often get cries for help from parents who want to see their teenagers grow spiritually and get involved at church, and a mentor can be helpful with this.

Your leaders need to know that this new resource will be available for students who could use more attention and care. Small group leaders sometimes end up with large numbers of students to shepherd, so some additional help can be great. A mentor can stay in touch with a student's small group leader and discover more about the student's needs and how to mentor him or her.

TIP

If you've coordinated your efforts well with your church's leadership, your new ministry will likely experience a positive introduction to the congregation.

Congregation

Let the congregation know that the program is beginning and ask that people prayerfully consider becoming a mentor. There will also be interest from parents who would like mentors for their teenagers. Be creative in how you "cast the vision" for your church. Use student testimonies, multimedia elements, and success stories from other mentoring programs.

Remember, the mentoring coordinator will quickly become the "cheerleader" for this new program. Be excited and enthusiastic about how God can use your mentors to multiply the impact of your youth ministry. Talk about the vision and be prepared to answer people's questions.

If you are the person leading this new ministry, you don't need to start with a fully formed program. Start small! Ask God to help you grow while the ministry is growing. Little-by-little can be a good thing. God's instructions are an example of this in Exodus 23:29-30. Through your total reliance upon God, the ministry will grow in his timing. It's better to start small and grow, than to over-commit on Day One and implode in the first six months.

Consider launching this new program with two people: You as the first mentor and one student as your mentee. You will learn a lot by mentoring a student yourself before you expand the program. Don't view your student as a test subject, of course, but take advantage of those first steps to see what works and what doesn't. This will help set you up to succeed as the program grows.

Perhaps you will recruit and train another mentor or two in this first stage, but we recommend against moving forward with a huge program at first. Be patient. It can be a slow process because much of it depends on scheduling times to meet with prospective mentors, interviewing them, and training them. It also takes time to interview and match up students. Follow God's timing because he will faithfully bring mentors and students together with a purpose.

TIP
Remember the principle Jesus shared in Luke 19:26. If you're faithful with what you've been given, God will trust you with more.

If you decide to mentor a student yourself, consider these steps. You'll see these ideas echoed later in this resource as we talk about getting other mentors involved in your program:

Talk With the Student
If you don't already know the student, call and set up a time to meet. This can just be a simple and brief meeting over sodas—or Starbucks, if you want to make it a little more fun. Talk to the student about what a mentor is and isn't. Your student will be glad to know that you will not be acting as another parent. Keep it light but be sure the student understands the commitments you're both making to the mentoring relationship.

So, what should you do next if the student indicates interest?

Meet the Parents
The purpose of this meeting is to get their permission and to let them know what they can expect from this relationship with their teenager. We recommend including the student in this meeting so there won't be any misunderstanding about the relationship. It also gives the parent and teenager a chance to discuss issues and ask questions together.

Meet at the church office or on the church campus. At this meeting, the parental permission form can be reviewed and signed, and you can give the parents a letter discussing expectations. (See the Parent Affirmation form on p. 130 and the Parent Letter on p. 131.) This is also a good time to figure out the best days and times for you and the student to meet. Exchange contact information, including phone numbers and email addresses, and set the first time you will meet with the student.

Hang Out Together
The first time you meet with the student, choose a place where you can have easy conversation (in other words, not a movie or concert or motocross event). This is when you can find out what issues the student would like help with and set some goals for personal or spiritual growth. Or maybe you'll find out the student has absolutely no goals and wants no help. That's OK—at least you have a place to start.

This is the time to introduce the Mentoring Covenant form (you'll find a copy on p. 118). This form will serve as a reminder of the anniversary date of when you and the student started the mentor relationship. It also will open the door for talking about the commitment each of you is making.

Don't worry if the student isn't overly helpful with this at first. It takes some students time to really open up. Trust is a big issue, and as your student gets to know you, he or she will be more comfortable talking about things.

Be Consistent
Now that you have started, make sure to meet weekly with your student; we recommend meeting for at least an hour. If either of you has a conflict with an upcoming date, make sure you communicate and reschedule.

Emails, text messages, and notes can help you stay in touch. The important thing is to be consistent. You may have to really pursue the student because some teenagers will be unsure about this new venture. It may take patience and persistence on your part. Just make sure to call, text, or email if you need to reschedule for a particular week.

Keep a journal (we've included one for you to print straight from the CD-ROM) to record your activities, prayer requests, and praises. This will help you remain focused on all the things God is doing in your student's life. It's also a great long-term resource that you will treasure as your mentoring relationship grows and matures.

Stay Connected to the Family
Contact your student's family as a courtesy to see how they view the mentor relationship, and let them know of your continued commitment. Remember, your job isn't to replace a parent; it's to come alongside the student's family and become a friend and role model and source of support. Anything that strengthens the parents and the family ultimately will strengthen the student, too.

TIP
Remember, you're launching a new program and heading into uncharted territory. Your student can't compare notes with peers, so that may be the source for some caution or reluctance.

You could write an entire book on the characteristics of a great mentor. In fact, we've read many of those very books! We simply want to share a few traits that we've seen in the healthiest mentors from our past experiences.

Consistency

Consistency isn't the same as perfection. Consistency means living a spiritually integrated life and avoiding spiritual compartmentalization—in other words, keeping God involved in every area of your life. Teenagers want to follow mentors who demonstrate consistency and integrity. They will have their eyes and ears open for major inconsistencies in the life of a mentor—or any other adult.

TIP

Consistency also means being consistent in your meeting schedule with your mentee. Lack of consistency here communicates lack of interest and lack of commitment.

Transparency

Don't try to act a certain way in the mentoring process. Be yourself and allow your teenager to see that you're a person who has good days and bad days. Don't attempt to become "cool," because most teenagers can see right through the act. Let your student discover what it means to be a genuine Christian—something that teenager will see in your life as you spend more and more time together.

TIP

Another reason mentors shouldn't attempt to become cool—most of us aren't! Maybe we were cool when we were 15 or 21 but not anymore! So why bother? Just be true to who you are today.

Good Listener

Good listening skills are important to the success of any relationship, including a mentoring relationship. Being a mentor doesn't mean imparting all of your wisdom and knowledge to a deserving young person. A good mentor will listen to the questions and hear what the teenager is saying, instead of trying to figure out what to say next. Listen!

Honesty

Honesty is so important in mentoring. A mentor might see something in the student's life that other people have been hesitant to say. A good mentor will talk about all areas and be honest with the mentee. Ultimately, honesty will provide a healthy foundation for your mentoring relationship.

Forgiving Attitude

Your student will fail you. You will fail your student. Neither of you is perfect. A healthy mentor accepts that fact and is willing to forgive and to seek forgiveness. Of course, this doesn't mean you shouldn't challenge your teenager to excel and work hard, but be patient as your student learns—and remember that forgiveness is a two-way street.

Encourager

Most teenagers today don't get enough encouragement. Some have good parents and friends who are encouraging, but as a whole, teenagers greatly lack in this area. A good mentor will encourage the student and find things in his or her life that are positive. Affirmation is one of the greatest ways to build bridges with teenagers. Learn to encourage more.

Faithful

Praying for your teenager should be a high priority as you develop and strengthen your mentoring relationship. Some weeks you may be praying about a specific challenge your student is facing. Some weeks you may be simply praying for wisdom or strength. Prayer changes things and allows the Holy Spirit to reveal things that you would not know otherwise. Commit to being a healthy mentor and pray daily for your student.

And let's be honest. Can any of us ever receive too much encouragement? We don't think so, either.

TIP

As a leader, your ministry will benefit if you're also praying daily—for your mentors, for your students, and for your families.

RECRUITING MENTORS
RUNNING THE PROGRAM

After you have begun the process of mentoring a student yourself, start looking for others who also would be willing to make this commitment to a student.

Where will you find these super humans who can persevere when they get no positive response, who do all the giving, who get "stood up" but keep trying, and who still have a heart for teenagers? All around you!

Recruiting is never a one-time event. It's an ongoing process for any ministry, and you'll face some unique challenges as you recruit people for your mentoring program. You're creating something new, so you can't point to a long list of volunteers at your church who've been involved in the past. You'll probably find that prospective mentors have lots of questions, and some may want to take small steps of commitment.

Can you remember what it was like to be a teenager? Do you remember an adult coming alongside you to help you through those tough years? Maybe you didn't have someone like that in your life but you wish a Christian mentor had been there for you.

It's not always easy to find mentors, but we've found God is faithful and will bring mentors when they are most needed. And it all seems to revolve around God's timing and purpose of matching them with the students that need mentors at the right moment.

Begin With Prayer

So, how do you find mentors? Prayer should always be your first step. Ask for God's guidance in leading you to the right people and leading the right people to your program. Don't take the "practical" steps without praying first.

Here's one "practical" way to discover quality mentors. Ask the teenagers in your youth ministry: "If you could spend an hour just asking questions and talking with someone who really gets it

TIP

This is a huge, important truth to grasp. Recruitment is a mentality—always looking for ways to help people get involved and serve God and others through the local church.

TIP

We know, we're beating the prayer drum. Working with teenagers can certainly be trying at times. Being in tune with God can help us adults be more effective with teenagers— especially when the going gets tough.

and lives a Christ-filled life, who would that be?" You may get two names or a list of 100, but these would be good people to pursue as possible mentors.

Another way to recruit is to have teenagers talk publicly about how mentoring—or simply the involvement of an adult—has changed their lives. This could happen in a weekend service or in a youth meeting. You could have students speak in front of the crowd, or you could create a video weaving together stories from several teenagers. When someone speaks passionately about mentoring, it can be a magnet that attracts other potential mentors.

Ask your current adult volunteers about people they would refer to the mentoring program. They'll probably recommend people they respect and enjoy being around. Most of us tend to hang around others with similar likes and interests, so your best leaders may be able to point you to others who could be good mentors.

Want some more options? Recruit in adult Sunday school classes or small groups, and if you have a program to help church members find their place of service, let that department know you are looking for mentors. Ask current mentors to recruit friends. Make some fliers or brochures that can be passed out at various places around church—at ministry fairs, in small groups, on an information table on the weekends, and so on.

There are people in your church who would be ideal mentors to your students—you just need to find them!

Don't Limit Your Options
Mentors come in all shapes, sizes, and ages—from a college student to a senior citizen. You might think most students would want a young, cool-looking mentor to hang out with. But you'd be surprised. Some of the best mentors will probably be more mature people who have experienced life and aren't too busy to spend

PEER-TO-PEER TIP
When recruiting teenage mentors, look for young people who have demonstrated a willingness and eagerness to serve. Your best mentors will probably be teenagers who have tasted the joy of serving God through ministry involvement.

TIP

This could be the source of some of your greatest mentors. God is always looking for ordinary people who are faithful and available and willing to serve. Offer some encouraging words to people who haven't seen themselves as servant leaders—even though God has called them to serve!

PEER-TO-PEER TIP

When evaluating the attitude and heart of a teenage mentor applicant, remember: You're looking for people who have displayed maturity and spiritual depth BUT this person is still a teenager, not an adult.

some time with a teenager. One of the greatest mentor relationships we've witnessed is between a senior citizen and teenage guy who's now a high school senior. They have met with each other every Saturday for the last three and a half years. Their relationship is steady, and this mentor has been a stabilizing force in this young man's relationship with his single-parent mother.

The best mentors are the ones who have the right attitude and heart. That's what matters—not their age, or what music they listen to, or what kind of car they drive, or how they dress.

And remember this: Every church has people who've never thought about what they could offer a teenager. Some are intimidated by the energy and unpredictability of students, but they would thrive in a one-on-one relationship. Others have made mistakes that could help your teenagers avoid similar hardships, but they don't know how to pass along this wisdom.

How do you recruit individuals in those categories? Consider holding an informal question-and-answer time that will allow them to hear your heart on teenagers and understand that they could make a difference in someone life. And it's worth repeating: Your existing relationships and your other leaders' existing relationships are often the best way to open these doors.

Personal relationships may open the best doors to the best mentors, but don't ignore the more impersonal options:
- Make an announcement in adult worship service.
- Place an announcement in the church bulletin or program.
- Use your church's website.
- Send an email to parents.

It's a challenge to keep a balance of mentors and students who need mentors, but God can handle that, too. It's better to have mentors waiting in the wings rather than having students on a waiting list for mentors, but that does happen. If you have mentors waiting for students, get them involved in helping at your weekend worship service or some other volunteer opportunity that keeps them connected to your students. They may just find a student to mentor as they serve in this other area.

So, once you have someone who shows interest, what's next?

SCREENING MENTORS AND OTHER LEGAL ISSUES
RUNNING THE PROGRAM

TIP

If there's any area of this process to make sure that you have all your bases covered, this is it. Screening your potential mentor candidates and making sure they are people of integrity is of utmost importance, especially when they will be in direct contact with teenagers.

PEER-TO-PEER TIP

Consider including a GPA requirement for teenage mentors. Don't make it unrealistic, like a 4.0. But if a student has a 1.8 GPA, this teenager may not be making the best choices and may not be your best choice for your mentoring ministry—not at the moment, anyway.

We believe a screening process is one of the keys to a healthy, effective mentoring program. As you begin the process, take time to pray over every prospective mentor. It's crucial to trust God throughout this process, and to ensure that you make wise decisions along the way. We all need God's help any time we're placing people into positions of leadership and responsibility. Remember, God knows what is inside every person's heart, and he may give you an internal "check" that tells you this person shouldn't be a mentor—maybe it's a timing issue, maybe it's a spiritual health issue. Or God will give you a clear sense that this person is a perfect fit for your program. Trust God and follow his lead when choosing mentors!

You'll come in contact with prospective mentors through a variety of ways. Have an initial phone conversation with each individual to talk about how the program works, the application and screening process, and the commitment each mentor is asked to make. If the person is still interested, get an application to him or her.

The Application

Your youth ministry may already have a volunteer application process; if so, we encourage you to use its application form. If you don't already have an application form and process, we've included a sample starting on p. 97 that can serve as a model as you create your own. The application should include two or three references for people who know the prospective mentor well. (See the Mentor Reference Form on p. 116.) It also would be wise to require a copy of the applicant's driver's license and proof of auto insurance.

Some prospective mentors who seem enthusiastic at the beginning of the process will drop out at this point and you may never see their application—that's OK. The individual may not have the time to commit to the program, or this person may not be willing to have you look further into his or her background. That's one of the reasons for using an application and interview process: multiple opportunities to weed out people who won't be a good fit or who just shouldn't be working with teenagers.

Go through the process with each person who does submit an application. Look through the application for any "red flags" that concern you. Call the references to discuss the applicant's ministry experience and personal strengths. In other words, do your homework. After all, families are entrusting their teenagers to your program!

Promptly schedule an interview with the applicant. If you're a man and the applicant is a woman (or vice versa), have another person present for the interview. And if you already have a team of leaders in place, having them involved in the interview can be beneficial, too.

The Interview

Plan on the interview taking approximately 60 to 90 minutes. A good location to meet is at the church office, but it can take place anywhere you won't be interrupted.

Your interviews will be great opportunities to learn more about your applicants and why they want to get involved in the mentoring program. Are they flexible? Can they handle rejection? Are they effective listeners? Do you have candidates with life experience that will match well with your students?

We've included a list of recommended questions in Part Two of this resource (see p. 109). We've included space after each question so you can write down the applicant's answers and other notes from the interview. If you don't have time for all of the situational questions, use the "leftovers" during the initial training time.

Explain your requirement that all mentors be fingerprinted and give the applicant the information on how to go about it. Explain the commitment you ask each mentor to make to the program. The applicant may want to pray about it and discuss it with family before committing. Give your applicant the Mentor Commitment

TIP
Having at least one other veteran leader with you for the interview is always a good idea. It provides you with additional accountability in case of conflict or disagreement, but it also provides a second source for questions you can ask the applicant.

PEER-TO-PEER TIP
Check with your local law enforcement agency and meet with your church leadership to discuss the best screening process for teenage mentors. You're placing minors into a role with responsibility, so be serious about this process.

Pray for the Holy Spirit to give you wisdom and discernment throughout the application and interview process. God sees everything in the applicant's life and can give you an internal "check" if something just isn't right.

PEER-TO-PEER TIP

Here are some "red flags" you might face with teenage mentor applications that are different from the ones you might see with adults. These aren't necessarily about the student's lifestyle. Some could be predictors of future problems:

1. Overly immature or rebellious attitude
2. Very new Christian (six months or less)
3. Inconsistent with current responsibilities
4. Strong opposition from parents
5. Too many commitments or areas of involvement already

form (see the sample on p. 115) to fill out and give to you if they are sure they are ready, or take it home and return to you after prayerful consideration.

If all goes well with the interview, the next step will be to schedule a time of initial training. But if you run into a "red flag" somewhere in the interview process, you'll need to intentionally slow things down.

Recognizing "Red Flags"

Here are some potential "red flags" that could disqualify a mentor applicant or could justify a slower process for getting that person involved.

1. Interested in opposite sex mentoring (could be called creepy)
2. Overly physical interactions with kids or teenagers, including same-gender interactions
3. Hesitant to submit to a background check
4. Overly busy
5. More than one strained relationship with family/friends
6. "Know-it-all" attitude or resistant to training
7. Negative or critical view about kids or teenagers
8. Not involved in the local church/not a church member
9. Been attending your church for a short period of time

Sometimes during the interview process, the prospective mentor will disqualify himself or herself, or the applicant will decide to wait. Again, that's a good thing. Our experience has been that God is faithful to do his own weeding out—and your interview and screening process will be an important part of that.

Saying "No" to an Applicant

No one likes being rejected or rejecting others—well, some people might enjoy it, but we don't think spiritually healthy people do! In order to keep your mentoring program positive and healthy, you may need to reject potentially bad mentors. We have already covered how to make good choices in choosing the right mentors. If you've determined that a mentor applicant will not make the cut, there are some things that you should know.

Make sure that you have said from the start that not everyone is admitted into the mentoring program. This is very important! Applicants need to understand that there are guidelines for selection and that you will follow these guidelines. This will enable you to break bad news gently, and it will allow mentors that are selected to feel a sense of accomplishment.

And as hard as it might be to honestly discuss your concern, it's much better to bring it up NOW than to be forced to address a problem down the road. If you have a minor concern about this person as a mentor, you could discuss the issue with the youth pastor or other members of your leadership team, and you may opt to redirect the person to be part of the youth ministry in another capacity where there might be a better fit or more supervision.

The best way to decline a potential mentor's application is to have a face-to-face conversation. This may not be easy, but honesty is always best. If the applicant asks for a clearer or more detailed explanation to know why you made your decision, then be prepared to discuss the guidelines and why he or she did not meet the criteria. Thank the applicant for participating in the interview and application process and be ready to suggest other opportunities to serve in your youth ministry or elsewhere in your congregation.

Remember: You will probably meet people who are at first very excited about mentoring, but for whatever reason they never end up mentoring. Usually, the process of interviewing and training mentors will naturally eliminate those who would not make good mentors. If a prospective mentor isn't patient and persevering enough to get through the process, it could indicate the person wouldn't have been a successful mentor.

PEER-TO-PEER TIP
If you believe a student isn't a good fit for your peer-to-peer program, look for a place for that teenager to serve on a student ministry team or some other opportunity in your youth ministry or church.

TIP
If you feel it's necessary, have another trusted volunteer or staff member in the room with you when you reject the candidate for the mentoring opportunity.

Info on Fingerprinting

It is vital that your screening process includes background checks and/or fingerprint submissions for prior arrest or conviction records. This will bring credibility and protection to your program. There are different ways for conducting the necessary background check. Your children's ministry may already have a system to screen volunteers that you can use. If not, check with your county or state authorities on their procedures. There are also organizations and ministries that facilitate screening for mentor programs, like www.churchvolunteercentral.com. Or, visit the Christian Association of Youth Mentoring (www.caym.org) for other suggestions.

FBI fingerprint checks often do not have records on low-level offenses, such as DUIs, so you may want to consider a driver's license check or a state criminal records check through your state agency, in addition to the fingerprint/background check.

You may also wish to do a child abuse registry check because some abuse cases are never prosecuted but still may be listed in the registry. Child abuse registries can be found on websites such as those found at www.familywatchdog.us and www.meganslaw.ca.gov.

After the background check is complete and references have been contacted, if the mentor is approved, it will be time for training.

TRAINING MENTORS
RUNNING THE PROGRAM

You can provide training for just one mentor at a time or for a group of prospective mentors. This initial training will take about two hours. Because most mentors will be working adults, this training session could be held on a weekday evening or a Saturday morning. It will provide a good foundation for getting a new mentor started.

Mentor Training Session
Here is some suggested content for this meeting.

- Opening
- "The How-To Booklet"
- "Things You and Your Teenager Can Do Together"
- "How to Share God with Your Teenager"
- "The Art of Asking Questions"
- "Helping Teenagers and Families in Crisis"
- "Mentoring Covenant"
- "Parent Affirmation"
- "Parent Letter"
- "Monthly Mentor Report"
- Ministry Journal
- Other Resources
- Questions & Answers / Commitment Form / Close in Prayer

Throughout the next few pages, we will attempt to give you an overview of these.

Opening
- Welcome everyone and get acquainted
- Icebreaker—Have mentors introduce themselves based on who they were as teenagers

Use this kind of opening as you welcome the mentors to the training session:

"God generally chooses people who think they are unqualified to do the job. Take Moses, for example. God wanted him to

TIP
Create a ministry opportunity for another leader by asking that person to coordinate snacks and beverages for your initial mentor team meeting.

PEER-TO-PEER TIP
Some of this content will be relevant for your teenage mentors. Consider a combined training session for adult and teenage mentors—and then divide the two groups to provide more specialized training for each group. Review each document carefully, because some may need to be revised for teenage mentors.

confront Pharaoh and to be the leader of his people, yet Moses felt hopelessly inadequate. He told God he got 'tongue-tied' and his words 'got tangled' (Exodus 4:10). But God wanted a person who would be totally dependent on him, so he chose Moses. In the same way, God chooses us to work with teenagers. None of us is highly qualified to become a mentor, but with God's help, we can be successful. If you feel inadequate, that's good! You are the type of person God is seeking."

With a few of these resources, we've provided a short explanation or introduction. All of the resources can be found in Part Two of this resource. Some require no explanation here, but take time BEFORE your training session to familiarize yourself with ALL of the materials.

"The How-To Booklet" (see p. 119)

"Things You and Your Teenager Can Do Together" (see p. 123)
I'm sure you're familiar with the goofy lists youth pastors come up with for wild and crazy things to do with students. Well, you can relax and just let your student be your guide. In this busy age, you could even just invite your mentee over to help you clean your garage or run errands with you on occasion. You don't need to spend lots of money, either—unless you make going to Starbucks a habit! Here's what one mentor and some students had to say about what they did together:

"Adapt to your kid. If your kid wants to talk, bike, watch a movie, play catch, or whatever—do it, especially early on. It's the time, not the activity that counts."

"I liked going to Golden Spoon (a frozen yogurt shop) with my mentor, going hiking, making my own earrings, sharing our free time, but also, of course, the talking was a very good thing."

"STARBUCKS! No, I loved everything that I did with Julie. She was just a really funny person, and she always did, well, ditzy things."

TIP

As your mentoring ministry grows, keep a log of the fun, creative ideas that your mentors have used. You'll be amazed at some of the low-cost, high-impact ideas that will make the list.

PEER-TO-PEER TIP

Create a student-focused version of this list that will fit within your parameters for teenage mentors.

"We loved eating! Selma's Chicago Pizzeria is where we loved eating. You can talk about anything while you eat and you still have enough time to go bowling or to a bookstore, or something. My favorite times were when we'd meet and get Starbucks and go to the church and just have good, fun girl-time while incorporating our Bible study, too."

"At first it was just awesome to go out and eat. To be honest, that is why I wanted to go with my mentor, Dave, in the first place, so that we could go out and get some good food. I did not eat out very much, because I am poorer, and so when Dave came around and we could go out to Del Taco or some other place to eat, it was really a treat for me! Eventually, things became more serious, and we spent more time together hanging out at his house playing with his kids, going to hockey games, or baseball games together. It was awesome to have Dave come out and support me at local events that I participated in, and it was really awesome when he was able to stop by when I had track meets or cross country meets. Just talking to him when I need him is also a huge, huge plus. So many memories. It was awesome how he was invited into my life, such as those track meets, and it was awesome when he invited me into his life, such as for his graduation party—so many things."

This handout includes a list of suggested activities for mentors.

"How to Share God with Your Teenager" (see p. 125)

"Helping Teenagers and Families in Crisis" (see p. 128)
It's important to prepare your mentors for possible crisis situations. Having some procedures in place will give them confidence to handle those tough times. And it's important for them to know that they will not handle them alone, but they will have your guidance and support.

Before you ever start the mentor program, decide the chain of command for these crisis situations. If you are the coordinator and a volunteer, you will certainly want to notify the youth pastor or staff when there is a situation of a serious nature going on with one of the mentored students. If your church has a counselor/therapist on staff or a counseling department, you may want to include them in that chain of command. Also, if lay counseling is available at your church, determine how you might refer parents and students, if they will provide counseling for them.

Right away, my team (Tami) was challenged with one of these tough situations. Shelley was a troubled student in a family with lots of challenges. Her mentor, Amber, had been spending time with her for a few months when Shelley said she needed to tell her something that Amber would need to keep a secret. That secret was that her father had sexually abused her in the past.

Lesson number one—**DO NOT ever tell a student you will keep a secret!** Before allowing the student to proceed, tell him or her that you may not be able to do that, depending on what is revealed. If it is something that is harmful to the student or another person, you will have to act on it. However, because you care so much for your student, you will be right there, helping him or her see it through.

In this situation, Amber called me and we discussed that Child Protective Services (CPS) would need to be notified. This was especially difficult because now Amber would have to tell Shelley's secret, and Amber was devastated by what this would do to their relationship. Plus, Amber had no idea whether Shelley's accusations were true.

If the situation calls for a report to CPS (or the appropriate authorities for your area), the ideal action to take is to make the call with the student. I (Tami) have found CPS to be very helpful, even just giving advice in other instances when we didn't know if a situation justified a report to them.

It was a very difficult period when both Shelley and her family were angry with Amber. But the family was now getting help. Child

Protective Services required the family get counseling and things were getting better. It didn't take long before Shelley and her family reconciled with Amber, and though Amber eventually moved to another part of the country, she and Shelley remain friends.

Lesson number two—**DO what's right even though it is difficult.** God can make good things come out of bad situations.

Take time during your training session to review the rest of the information in this resource. Don't assume that your mentors already know this information. Be sure your mentors know that they should contact you immediately with any problems of a serious nature. And make sure they also have contact information for someone else on the youth ministry/church staff in case you are not available. They need to know that they will not be alone in tough circumstances, and you need to know what is happening with these students and their families.

More commonly, there will be times when parents and a student clash or they are having problems communicating. It is important for the mentor not to get in the middle. However, sometimes it is unavoidable and there may be an opportunity for the mentor to be a peacemaker.

This is exactly how God has used Jose in the life of his student, Mike. Jose has acted as a "relief valve" in the life of Mike and his single-parent mom. Jose reminds Mike of how his mother feels stressed and tired when she gets home from work, and that some understanding and a clean house go a long way toward peace in the home. And it seems that Jose's presence in Mike's life is a stabilizing force, helping mom to see a few things Mike's way, too.

It is great to have someone on your leadership team who has experience counseling youth. That person can be a great support to the mentors when they have minor things come up and need some advice on possible solutions.

TIP
It's best to assume that your mentors have no idea how to respond to these crisis situations. Overload them with information—not to make them feel overwhelmed but to help prepare them for possible situations down the road. And remind them that there will always be help with difficult situations.

TIP
It's important that mentors understand that they should never take sides or speak negatively about a mentee's family member(s).

"Mentoring Covenant" (see p. 115) (Adapted from an out-of-print resource, *One Kid at a Time*)
The Mentoring Covenant is a commitment that the mentor and student make together. This should be done one of the first times that they meet. It will let the student know that the mentor is serious about his/her commitment and that the mentor expects a level of commitment from the student.

It will also serve as a reminder of their "anniversary" at the end of the commitment, at which time they can re-evaluate their mentoring relationship and decide on any continued commitment.

Our experience shows that many mentor relationships will continue on indefinitely. Many mentors will make such a solid bond with the student and the family that the relationship will go on beyond the student's high school years, without the formal commitment and umbrella of the church. As one student commented to her mentor, "I expect you to mentor my own children someday."

On the other hand, there will be those mentor relationships that last just for the formal commitment. Here's what one mentor had to say about her experience:

"My student eventually joined a small group, which her mother and I had been encouraging her to do, and she became involved in mission trips, and became too busy for the mentoring program. But I think that perhaps I was there for her until she felt ready to become more involved in the church. This perhaps is one of the roles of mentors for teenagers that are shy and new to the church."

God has a purpose for every mentoring relationship. No two will be alike. We must trust that God is working out his purpose even when we can't see it.

TIP

Encourage your mentors to think about the legacy they're passing on to their students—and to young people one or two generations down the road!

PEER-TO-PEER TIP

This can happen with your peer-to-peer program, too. After graduating from high school, your teenage mentor may want to continue meeting with the younger student or connect with a different teenager. Be prepared for this transition, and have the mentor complete the necessary paperwork, screening, and training at this stage.

"Parent Affirmation" (see p. 130) (Adapted from *One Kid at a Time*)
The Parent Affirmation is basically a permission form for a parent or guardian to sign before the mentor and student start meeting. Because mentoring is a one-on-one relationship, it is very important to have the trust of the parents. They need to be confident that mentors are carefully screened and chosen. And they need to know that you are serious about your responsibilities as a mentor/program coordinator.

The ideal time to have the Parent Affirmation signed is when the student, the mentor, the program coordinator, and a parent or guardian have their initial meeting. This is a time of introduction for everyone. It can be done at the church office or another convenient place at a time when all can meet.

"Parent Letter" (see p. 131) (Adapted from *One Kid at a Time*)
The Parent Letter gives credibility to the program and provides guidelines for parents. If they know what to expect, they can be of support. Mentors are not substitute parents and should not be a threat to the parents. Mentors should be a friend of the family as well as the student.

See the section on "Matching Students with Mentors" on p. 60 for a full discussion of this initial meeting. The Parent Affirmation and Parent Letter are both important elements in that meeting.

"Monthly Mentor Report" (see p. 136)
This is an important piece to your program—it will help the leadership team keep a watch on each match and provide ongoing support as needed to the mentors and mentees. This is a catalyst for conversation and prayer between the coordinator and/or coaches and mentors on a monthly basis.

As stated by the National Mentoring Center (www.nwrel.org/mentoring), "All the effort that went into recruiting participants, delivering pre-match training, and making appropriate matches will be wasted if your program does not provide ongoing support and supervision. Your supervision and monitoring process should ensure a) the safety of meeting locations and circumstances; b) that matches have resources and materials for activities; c) continuing training opportunities and peer-support; d) assistance to mentors and mentees in negotiating and achieving goals; e) management of grievances and offering positive feedback; and f) ensure that appropriate documentation is done on a regular basis."

Ministry Journal

We'd encourage you to keep a journal while serving as a mentor. It's a great way to see how God is working in the life of your student. It can be an encouragement to see the steps the student has taken forward when he/she is struggling. Growth is normally slow and subtle, so looking back in your journal will help a mentor see that growth. Seeing small victories enables us to go forward with more courage and faith. Also, if the student being mentored has a lot of issues, it is a good idea to keep a record of dates and events in that student's life in case something of a serious nature comes up in the future. Be sure this journal is kept private.

Other Resources

This category can include anything that you feel may be of interest to mentors as they nurture their students. Some ideas: workbooks on how to manage their money, set goals, prepare for college or a job, or grow in their faith.

If a student is open to working with his or her mentor on some serious growing, you might want to check out a workbook entitled, *Successful Youth Mentoring: 24 Practical Sessions to Impact Kids' Lives* (Group Publishing). Some of the sessions (volumes 1, 2, and 3) include "Personality Strengths and Abilities," "Making the Right Decisions for the Right Reasons," "Anger," "Jealousy," "Global View," and "Purity." The workbooks also include practical helps for mentors.

One resource of particular significance for students with lots of hurts in their lives is *Life Hurts God Heals* (Simply Youth Ministry). This is an eight-step, 13-week program for students who are hurting because of addictions, abuse, dysfunctional families, depression, or any other kind of hurt. Although a student normally goes through this program in a group setting, the mentor can use this as a reference resource for the types of life problems the teenager is facing, and then encourage the student to join a group, even going with the student. Mentors also could use the curriculum individually with their students.

Questions & Answers / Commitment Form / Close in Prayer
Close your initial training session by answering people's questions. Also, explain the process from there—matching them with a student. This process may take some time. Mentors may want to consider serving as a general volunteer or some similar role where they will interact with students while they are waiting. This could also lead to a connection with a student who may want or need a mentor.

This initial meeting is a good time to present your commitment form to the prospective mentors, emphasizing that they should be very certain about their commitment. Give them an "out" if they have concerns or doubts. Sometimes you will have prospective mentors who are unsure about whether they can commit to the time or have some other concern. It's OK to ask them to wait and to let you know when they feel they can make a definite commitment. It's always rough when you match a student with a mentor who ends up being inconsistent.

When closing, pray that God will work in his perfect timing to bring about a match for these prospective mentors.

TIP
Keep track of the questions people ask at the end of this initial meeting. You may want to incorporate this information the next time you make a presentation to prospective mentors.

Ongoing Training

You'll find lots of value in regularly scheduled times for mentors to get together—quarterly or every other month or so. Just as parents of teenagers need support, so do mentors! If your youth ministry volunteers gather on a regular basis, the mentors can meet with them for part of the time and then break off for some "mentor time" to bounce ideas off each other, offer encouragement, and take advantage of more training.

Meeting with the whole team of youth ministry volunteers is a great way for the mentors to get to know the other youth volunteers and the programs and resources available. Our experience showed that most of the mentored students were not yet involved with the mainstream youth group. So, it's good for the mentors to know what's happening in the youth group so they can encourage their students to get involved. Sometimes the mentored students will get more connected, with encouragement from their mentor. This is a good goal to strive for, but it shouldn't be the primary purpose of a mentoring relationship.

Include time for fellowship and prayer. It can lead to good sharing when mentors help each other with suggestions and helpful tips. A word of caution: Mentors should be cautious about what information they share from or about their students. Speaking negatively about the student or his or her parents could be devastating to the relationship. Remind the mentors when they meet about the value of confidentiality with their students; they should be careful what they share in the group, using only first names of the students, and the issues discussed and information shared should never leave the group.

PEER-TO-PEER TIP
As you train and coach your teenage mentors, strike a healthy balance between general knowledge that all young mentors need and specific ways to assist that particular mentor. Each teenager is a unique person with unique needs, skills, talents, abilities—and weaknesses!

It is also good during mentor meetings to provide additional training. There are many great resources for additional training. Some were mentioned in the introduction chapter. Topics for additional training could include healthy boundaries with mentees, communication tips, how to handle conflict with your student, setting goals, working with parents, and so on.

TIP
Ask your mentors where they want or need training. Within a few weeks, they'll probably start to recognize areas where they'd like to become better equipped and more effective.

TIP

As you develop high-quality mentors, empower them to recruit other people from your congregation to get involved in this ministry.

PEER-TO-PEER TIP

We can't tell you the specific formula for determining if a student would benefit more from an adult mentor or a teenage mentor. But because we encourage a gap of at least three years between the student and mentor in a peer-to-peer program, you probably want to focus more on students between grades 6 and 9.

In most cases, students (or their parents) will find you! Word of mouth is probably your most effective advertising tool. You might get your first referrals from your youth pastor or an adult volunteer, or it could be a worried parent. Other times it will be a needy student without an involved parent. Or you may get a phone call from an interested parent who hears about the program through another parent whose child has a mentor.

You might think the best place to find students would be within your high school ministry—announcements during the weekend worship times or during small group times. Interestingly enough, this isn't always the case. We found that the students who were eager for a mentor when they first heard about it through the high school ministry were often already involved in lots of activities and ended up being too busy to meet with a mentor. That doesn't mean you shouldn't try to interest these already involved and active-in-the-ministry students. But be prepared: They may not have the time or interest level to make a mentor relationship work in the long run.

So make announcements and distribute brochures during the weekend worship times. And be prepared to respond to their interest. Check out the Application for a Mentor for interested students (see p. 134). This can help you assess why a student wants a mentor, specific areas where a mentor could assist, what kinds of school or community activities the student is involved in, and some of his or her personality traits.

If you have a reluctant student, consider using the application as a basis for an initial conversation; that student doesn't necessarily need to fill it out and return it. It may take several phone calls or a face-to-face meeting to help a reluctant student understand what having a mentor is all about and to encourage that teenager to give it a try. We recommend that the coordinator or one of the team leaders or coaches be the person to have these conversations with a reluctant student.

We talked to a few mentored students to get some advice they would give another student considering having a mentor:

"Get one. Trust me on this one. If you don't find a mentor that fits right for you, then you can tell them. But having a mentor there is awesome. Take this example: When you are having a fight with your parents, how awesome would it be that you could call another adult and tell him/her your side of the story, and see it from a third point of view. Maybe that doesn't work for you, but trust me. If you are thinking about having a mentor, get one!"

"It's not so bad—it's actually a lot of fun so just give it a chance. You'll never know what kind of friendship you'll gain if you don't. Having a mentor was a big blessing in my life as a teenager. I struggled a lot and was tempted a lot, too. Maybe if I hadn't had a mentor in my life I wouldn't have chosen the right path. Starting in the beginning of high school I pretty much stopped going to church, but I still was a follower."

"Open up. You think you don't want one but it's like your own personal best friend who you don't have to share with anyone else."

God has an incredible way of helping balance the number of students with the available mentors, in most cases. If you do happen to get a bunch of students who want mentors but no mentors are available, encourage the students to join a small group or find another way to get connected with the youth ministry while they are waiting for mentors.

TIP

A reluctant student who is being pushed by a parent to have a mentor will need to be persuaded to give it a try. However, if the teenager refuses, he or she shouldn't be forced—and probably can't be. Our experience has been that those types of relationships don't work.

The Application for a Mentor

The Application for a Mentor form (see p. 134) can be used by the coordinator to collect the information on students that will be helpful in matching them with mentors. Some students will eagerly fill it out and return it to the coordinator, while the less eager participants may need encouragement from parents or program leaders.

If a student has to wait for a mentor (there are none waiting in the wings) you can use this opportunity to see if he or she is interested in joining a small group or another teenage ministry offered at your church. One goal of mentoring is to help get a student integrated into the youth ministry if he or she is not already involved, so this can be an effective step until a mentor becomes available.

In most cases the coordinator will use the student's application as a guide when meeting with the student or parent. Besides the normal contact information, it is helpful to know if the student attends weekend worship services or a small group, and where this teenager is spiritually. Is the student involved in any school or community activities? What does the teenager do for fun or in his or her free time? Try to learn something about the teenager's personality traits. And why is this student interested in having a mentor, or how might a mentor benefit this teenager? Of course, if this is the parents' idea, that question will be answered from their view of why they think their teenager needs a mentor.

The Match

We wish there was an exact science to this matchmaking, but it's often a "God thing." Sometimes, it will be apparent that God has a match in mind because the mentor's life experience will perfectly fit the student. Other times you won't see an immediate connection, but God will lead you in making the right match.

Sometimes students (or parents) will request a young college-aged mentor, thinking that the student will relate best if the mentor is closer to the student's age. Our experience shows this isn't always the case. Students seemed to benefit most from mentors with more life experience and more time to dedicate to the mentoring relationship.

As you look through your information, pay attention to life experience, availability, and geographics—in other words, will it be logistically easy or difficult for this mentor and this student to meet together. Examine your options, talk to your team, and spend time praying about it. Then make your match.

This is really important: Don't surprise the mentor with a student you haven't already discussed. You should have a profile with information on the student that you can discuss with the prospective mentor.

There may be circumstances that prevent a mentor from agreeing to a particular student. Perhaps the times a student might be available do not coincide with the mentor's schedule, or maybe personalities don't match, or something unexpected happens in the life of the mentor or student that causes a delay.

TIP
A delayed pairing is always better than an unhealthy or mismatched pairing.

Let God guide you in those times. Accept delays. They can be God's way of bringing the right mentor and student together at the right time. It's all about God's timing!

Meeting for the First Time
Once the mentor has accepted the assignment, make the introductions. Find a time when the student and at least one parent can meet with you (the coordinator) and the mentor for about 30 minutes. The best place to meet might be at the church office.

Although you have some pretty important stuff to discuss at this meeting, you want to keep it light. After the introductions, let the mentor tell the student about himself or herself. Since you

TIP
Humor is a great friend in this kind of situation, but it's always best to avoid humor that comes at the expense of an individual—whether that's you, the mentor, or the student.

will already know something about the student via the student application form, you or the mentor can break the ice with conversation about his or her interests.

The coordinator can use this time to have the parent fill out the Parent Affirmation form (see p. 130). Ask the parent to fill it out as best as possible while there, and be sure that you get it back.

This is also the time to give the Parent Letter (see p. 131) to the parent, stressing a couple of the main points in that letter. Remind both the student and parent that even though confidentiality is important in the mentor relationship, parents will be notified if the mentor is informed or aware of certain serious things, such as evidence that the student may harm herself or himself or others.

Give the Mentoring Covenant (see p. 118) to the mentor, and let the student know the length of the commitment the mentor is making. It is a serious commitment on the student's part, too. They should stick to the planned meeting times as much as possible, and the teenager should always let the mentor know if they need to reschedule. The mentor can use the form at their first meeting to discuss some goals and reconfirm the commitment. The form can then be kept by the mentor as a reminder of that anniversary. And—who knows—the student may want a copy, too.

Also, tell the student in the presence of the mentor that if for some reason he or she doesn't think it's a good match, the student should contact you and you will find another mentor. It's important for the teenager to hear this information so he or she won't feel trapped in this new thing. However, encourage the student to give it a good try of meeting at least a few times.

End by exchanging contact information, including email addresses and best times to meet. Be sure to have the mentor and teenager arrange the date and time for their first meeting before they leave.

Then, close in prayer—and keep praying for this match in the days ahead.

BEYOND MATCHMAKING
RUNNING THE PROGRAM

TIP

As you gain more experience with the matches and the mentoring ministry, the tough situations will cause you less anxiety.

TIP

Besides monthly reports from mentors, the coordinator should check with the parents quarterly to be sure things are on track.

Within a couple weeks of a student and mentor match, be sure to check with the mentor to evaluate their progress. Are the mentor and teenager meeting regularly? How are things going?

Sometimes it is a challenge to get the mentor relationship off the ground. Some students wonder just what they got themselves into—or what their parents got them into—and they may not be eager for the phone to ring with that first mentor call. It's not unusual for a student and mentor to have problems connecting at first, so don't panic.

Your job is to encourage the mentor to keep on pursuing the student. Note these comments from a student—a very insightful one—in this regard:

"Keep it up. When your mentee who normally is calling you every week hasn't called in a month, call or send an email asking, 'Hey, what's up?' If you are with someone who has a similar interest, open up with that. Starting off in a mentoring relationship is hard stuff. It is going to take a lot of care and time and attention in the beginning to set the roots firm. Keep up the relationship, and remember that your mentee is a person as well. Sure, he/she hopefully will open up his/her life to you, but don't feel afraid to open up your life to them! Mentees need to know that it is safe for them to be open and honest, and the only way for them to know that is if you are open and honest."

If the mentor says the student is not returning phone calls, you can help by calling the student to see how things are going. It things aren't "going" at all, use your phone call to see how you can assist. Find out if there's genuine miscommunication between student and mentor or if it's a simple issue of "phone tag." Your nudge can make a difference in getting the ball rolling again with a call to action by one of the parties.

No Match

Occasionally, the match just isn't going to work. It is important to cover this possibility in the mentor training. Sometimes a student just doesn't have the time to add another commitment, or for whatever reason, the mentor and student just don't "click." In that case, have separate conversations with the student and the mentor.

If the student just doesn't want to commit to being mentored, you can talk with him or her about getting involved at another point down the road. Keep the conversation upbeat. You don't want to make the student feel guilty. Talk with that student's parents so they will be aware of the situation. It will also be important to find another student for the mentor, who is probably frustrated and possibly dejected.

On the other hand, if the mentor seems to be the uncommitted one, have a frank discussion with that mentor, suggesting he or she step back and re-evaluate whether this is really the right ministry opportunity. Then, do not delay in finding another mentor for that student. Again, keep the parents informed.

We've witnessed God provide just the right solution for these situations. Although it was disappointing at the time, when another match started up, it was always a blessing to see God at work in the new mentor relationship.

Resolving Conflict

In addition to poor matches or an uncommitted participant, mentoring relationships sometimes fall apart because of conflict. It may be caused by the mentor, or it may be caused by the student. Your primary goal is to help resolve the issue and then determine if the mentoring relationship can continue.

We encourage you follow a similar pattern to what we discussed above. Meet separately with the mentor and the student to

PEER-TO-PEER TIP
You may discover that some mentor-student matches don't work because of teenage peer dynamics that you wouldn't discover in an adult-teenager match. That's OK. Pray about it, encourage reconciliation, and be prepared to make a different match.

TIP
When it comes to parents, we have three recommended policies.
1. Communicate.
2. Communicate.
3. Communicate.
Seriously. We don't think it's possible to overcommunicate with parents!

determine the source of the conflict and how much the relationship has been affected. If you, as the leader, feel that it is something small that they can overcome, then consider bringing them both together and serving as a mediator. If the conflict seems to be a major hurdle, the best solution probably is to find a more suitable mentoring partner for each person. But even if ending the partnership is the ultimate decision, encourage them to find some form of resolution—after all, that's the biblically right thing to do!

Reaching Closure

Set up a system—you could use Outlook Calendar or some other software program—to be reminded of when the commitment period is about to end for each mentoring partnership.

As that date approaches, you need to answer an important question: Now what? The student and mentor should discuss whether they want to continue in the formal mentoring relationship. The coordinator can help them through the process. Even if they decide to end the formal mentor relationship, it doesn't necessarily mean the end to their friendship. If there has been real bonding, they will naturally stay in touch—maybe for a lifetime.

If the formal relationship is ending, a brief, informal, confidential exit interview will help the coordinator evaluate the program, and it will help the mentor and teenager end on a positive note. Ask the **teenager** questions such as:

- What kinds of things did you enjoy doing with your mentor?
- Did you set any goals? Were they achieved?
- Did it help you to have a mentor? How?
- What advice would you give new mentors?
- What advice would you give a friend considering a mentoring relationship?

The **mentor** also should be encouraged at this time. It is sometimes hard for a mentor to see growth in a student, and you may be able to help the mentor see that growth has happened, after you get feedback from the student. Ask questions such as:

- What worked and didn't work with your student?
- How was your communication with the parent(s)?
- What did you and your mentee learn from each other?
- What suggestions do you have for other mentors?
- Are you ready to mentor another student?

Don't leave out the **parent(s)**! They need to know if the formal mentoring relationship will continue or come to a close. Ask for their feedback, as well:

- What growth, if any, did you see in your child through this relationship?
- Did you feel like the mentor was a friend to your whole family?
- Do you have any suggestions for improving the program?

Keeping Good Records

We encourage you to keep a file on each mentor and student match. The folder can include the mentor's application and other background documents, the student application, and the start date of the match. Be sure to record notes of updates on each as well as collecting Monthly Mentor Reports from the mentor and/or their coach.

Because it contains personal information, this kind of file shouldn't be left in an easily accessible location. Use a locked file cabinet in a locked office. This is a good policy to follow for any applications: leadership team, mission trips, and so on.

PEER-TO-PEER TIP
Consider asking the parents of the teenage mentor for feedback, too.

TIP
Treat other people's private data and information with the same level of security and respect you'd like your own files to be treated. (Consider this the Golden Rule of privacy and respect!)

Your mentors are making a commitment of time, energy, and prayer. You have the opportunity—and obligation—to make a commitment to them. The more you value and encourage your mentors, the more they will love what they do and the more they will tell other people about their positive experiences in your program. There's no end to the list of ways to encourage people, but we want to highlight a few of the methods we've found to be most effective.

Food

Have food available at any training or informational meetings. This may seem trivial but everyone enjoys a snack, and it's a tasty way of saying "thanks." You also can invite mentors over to your house for a meal, or grab a bite together after a weekend church service. Food has the remarkable ability to rally a team together for a common cause.

Notes, Cards, and Gifts

Write notes of encouragement and thanks during the mentoring program. Sometimes a mentor may not feel a strong connection to the student, or the mentor may feel underappreciated. Your notes will help remind them why they're involved. A small token of your appreciation would be another final way to value your mentors. It doesn't have to be an expensive gift; truly, it's the thought that counts.

Public Recognition

Ask your senior pastor for a window of time at a weekend service to publicly thank your mentors. Incorporate them into volunteer appreciation events. Mention them as examples of people serving in your church. Bring them up to the stage during a youth service. Present them with a fun trophy or certificate after the first round of the program. In other words, find a way to publicly recognize their hard work and commitment without embarrassing them—unless they enjoy being embarrassed.

PEER-TO-PEER TIP

A gift card to a local restaurant, electronics store, or mall could be more meaningful to a teenage mentor than almost any other gift you could give!

TIP

Don't go buy new trophies. Hit up garage sales and thrift stores to find old, unwanted trophies. Then buy replacement pieces for the top of the trophies to make them unique and special.

Your Time

As your program grows, you might find it more challenging to spend time with individual mentors. Keep this a priority. Your mentors need you, as much as the students need their mentors. Once you've developed a coaching system, you'll have others who are investing in your mentors, but even then, continue looking for ways to spend time with your mentors—they know how valuable your time is, so they'll appreciate your investment.

Team Celebration

Come together as a team after the mentors and students have completed the final week of the program, whether it's been a year or just 10 weeks. This event can be a swimming party or an ice cream social or some other fun, creative celebration. Invite all the mentors and students. During your party, encourage people to share highlights. This is a very inspiring time for everyone, and it also helps to promote and continue the program. A final evaluation could be completed or handed out during this time. If it seems appropriate have cards available for mentors to sign up for the program's next round.

It's important that all parties involved in the mentoring process—youth ministry leaders, mentors, parents, and students—have realistic expectations about the results. A mentored student may not be ready to join in on every youth ministry event. The family may not see overnight change, and the student may not show immediate appreciation to their mentor or become a loving and obedient teenager at home.

Then again, it just might happen.

What expectations should you and your team have for this new mentoring program? According to a Child Trends Research Brief:

"Mentoring programs that are driven more by the needs and interests of youth—rather than the expectations of the adult volunteers—are more likely to succeed. Programs based on a 'developmental' approach to mentoring, instead of a 'prescriptive' approach, tended to last longer and be more satisfying for both mentor and mentee. In the developmental approach, mentors spent a lot of time initially getting to know their mentees, were flexible in their expectations of the relationships, and took their cues about what activities they would engage in with their mentees from the youth themselves. In the prescriptive approach, mentors viewed their goals for the match as paramount and required the youth to take equal responsibility for maintaining the relationship and assessing how it was working out."

Expect God to work in these mentoring relationships. Trust God to work in the lives of the young people you mentor. You are available, but God does the work.

Evaluate the program based on the exit reviews and feedback you receive from church staff, parents, mentors, and students. Are more students involved in the program? Did you see more adults become mentors? Do you have a larger crop of students and/or mentors for the next year? Did the students value the mentoring relationships?

TIP

Be realistic about your expectations, but maintain a positive, hopeful attitude for the mentoring ministry. That attitude will spread to the people around you.

PEER-TO-PEER TIP

As you develop your program, you'll gain a clearer sense of what results and progress is "normal" for your students. Keep track of these standards for future rounds of mentoring.

Do you have testimonies of students or mentors who've been impacted by the program? Make changes where needed, but most of all, depend on God to give you the wisdom to lead this program. The success is up to him.

CONCLUSION

TIP

Consider partnering up with other churches in your community for a collaborative effort. Or encourage other congregations to launch their own mentoring ministries. Create a network of ministries and leaders that can support each other!

PEER-TO-PEER TIP

Continue to invest in the lives of your teenage mentors and their younger mentees. Remember: These young people aren't just the church of tomorrow. They're the church of today—and you're helping them grow as leaders and followers of Christ!

This is just the beginning! Mentoring is alive and well and growing in our communities. The difference we can make as a faith community is huge—sometimes in large numbers and sometimes through the deep impact on a handful of lives. Sharing our faith and living authentic lives around our young people can bring purpose and hope to them—thanks to the power of God working through mentoring relationships.

We pray that you and many other people in your church experience the joy of showing God's love to students by spending time with them one-on-one and investing in their lives. Mentoring on purpose will produce God-sized results if we are willing to make the effort. Be passionate about seeing teenagers grow in their faith. Remain committed to developing a quality youth ministry. Stir up the excitement for seeing young people discover God's purpose for their lives.

Continue the story by multiplying the impact of your youth ministry! The second half of this book is filled with several editable forms, letters, sample curriculum, and more to help you get your mentoring ministry going!

PART 2
RESOURCES AND TOOLS

TABLE OF CONTENTS

PART TWO — PRACTICAL TOOLS AND RESOURCES

PURPOSE STATEMENT AND GUIDELINES

Sample Purpose Statement

*"Our mentoring program exists to support and challenge students, on a one-to-one basis and over time, to **GROW** in maturity and in their faith, to help them **DISCOVER** God's purpose and ministry for their lives, bringing **HONOR** to God."*

Mentors will "be there" for students—caring for them, guiding them, being a role model, and encouraging them.

Students who request mentoring or come to us as a result of parents' requests or youth ministry staff referrals will be brought to the attention of the mentoring coordinator(s). Students will be paired with mentors with an attempt to match interests, life experience, geographical location, and so on.

When a church member indicates a desire to serve as a mentor, he or she will be asked to fill out an application. The application will be used to screen the mentor and identify his or her interests and abilities that would be useful for matching the applicant with a student. After the required interview and reference and background checks are complete, the mentor will go through an initial training and then be matched with a student. Mentors will be asked to make a commitment of at least one year to the program.

Mentors will need the approval and support of parents, and cannot and should not take the place of parents. The mentor coordinator will meet initially with the parent(s), mentor, and student to explain the purpose of the mentoring relationship, obtain the permission of the parent, and schedule a first meeting for the student and mentor. A parent will be required to sign a Parent Affirmation form, giving permission for the relationship and giving emergency information and other important data.

The mentor will discuss with the student the commitment involved (both ways) in the mentoring relationship, decide on a regular time to meet, and set some goals they can accomplish together. A Mentoring Covenant can be signed between mentor and student, indicating their commitment.

Mentors are expected to attend the youth ministry volunteer staff meetings for ongoing support where they can voice their concerns and receive encouragement and prayer from each other. Also, additional training can be accomplished during the meetings.

The coordinator will have a team to assist with the various responsibilities of the mentor program.

The mentoring coordinator and team will be available to provide advice and information for the mentors and encourage them. They will also be available to the parents of the mentored teenagers if the need arises.

ICEBREAKER QUESTIONS
FOR MENTORS

It's important for mentors and mentees to get off on the right track when meeting, especially at the beginning of the relationship. Here are some sample icebreaker questions that can help get your session started.

- What animal would you be and why?

- What is the most beautiful or meaningful gift you've ever received?

- If you could have an endless supply of any food, what would you request?

- What is one big goal you'd like to accomplish during your lifetime?

- When you were little, who was your favorite superhero and why?

- Who is your hero now? (It could be a parent, a celebrity, an influential person in one's life, and so on.)

- What's your favorite thing to do in the summer?

- If they made a movie of your life, what would it be about and which actor would you want to play you?

- If you were an ice cream flavor, which one would you be and why?

- What's your favorite cartoon character and why?

- If you could visit any place in the world, where would you choose to go and why?

- What's your dream job, and why?

- Are you a morning or night person?

- What are your favorite hobbies?

- What are your pet peeves?

- What's the weirdest thing you've ever eaten?

- Name one of your favorite things about someone in your family.

- Tell me about a unique or quirky habit of yours.

- If you had to describe yourself using three words, what three words would you pick?

- If someone made a movie of your life would it be a drama, a comedy, a romantic-comedy, action film, or science fiction?

- What is your greatest fear?

SAMPLE 10-WEEK STUDY

Below, we have given you 10 topics that mentors can use when meeting with students. Using a pre-selected study can be helpful if you're using a shortened schedule for your mentoring program or if you're including a peer-to-peer option. Because you know your teenagers better than we do, we encourage you to select the best study or book for your mentor and mentee to go through. If you're not sure where to start, consider some of the studies we've included for you here. The content we've provided is loose, conversational-style material. We haven't provided you with a word-for-word script or even an outline. Instead, we've given you a few questions or ideas to share with your teenager to help guide your discussion. If something doesn't fit, change it! If your conversation goes down a healthy rabbit trail, follow it! Remember, this study is more about growing a trusting, Jesus-centered relationship with your teenager than sticking to a particular curriculum.

Here are the 10 topics we've included in this resource:

- Absolute Truth
- Encouragement
- Family Relationships
- Friendship
- Identity
- Opposite Sex
- Others First
- Struggles/Adversity
- Wise Choices
- You Are Gifted

C.A.P.S.

The acronym CAPS—Challenge, Affirm, Prayer, and Scripture—provides a structure for each of these 10 topics. Mentors don't have to always begin with the "Challenge," of course. Sometimes that will be the best place to start and other times it might need to be last.

Challenge

Mentors will challenge their mentees to live life to the fullest. They will address specific areas of life where God can help them grow. Mentees will be challenged and stretched during their time together.

Affirm

Mentors will look for ways to affirm the mentees. Every person does things well, and mentors will find these areas and encourage the mentees to continue to excel in these areas. Affirmation is an important ingredient in the mentoring relationship.

Prayer

Mentors will ask for prayer needs and pray with the mentees each week. They will commit to pray for each other and write down the requests to discuss them at the next meeting. Mentors should pray daily for the mentees.

Scripture

Mentors will have verses from the Bible to discuss with the mentees each time they examine one of the 10 topics. Mentees will be encouraged to memorize Scripture—and mentors are encouraged to learn the verses, too!

ABSOLUTE TRUTH

Of the 10 topics, this one might be the most challenging one for many teenagers. The topic is important because it needs to be foundational in your mentee's life. Satan will attack this foundation. Make sure you study your Scripture for this week so you grasp what it is addressing.

Challenge:
- What do you think "absolute truth" is? [Truth that is true, no matter what.]
- What is absolutely true to you?
- How can you share the absolute truth with others?

Affirm:
- I see you living a life that reveals the truth.
- Your lifestyle shows me you believe.

Prayer:
- How can I pray for you?
- Is there someone we can pray for who doesn't believe in absolute truth?

Scripture:
Jesus told him, "I am the way, the truth, and the life. No one can come to the Father except through me" (John 14:6).

"When the Spirit of truth comes, he will guide you into all truth. He will not speak on his own but will tell you what he has heard. He will tell you about the future" (John 16:13).

For in Christ lives all the fullness of God in a human body (Colossians 2:9).

So the Word became human and made his home among us. He was full of unfailing love and faithfulness. And we have seen his glory, the glory of the Father's one and only Son (John 1:14).

ENCOURAGEMENT

This week you can make an impact on your student by offering encouragement and helping him or her to encourage others. You may have to look for ways to encourage your mentee if you've just begun meeting recently. Remember, you will make a difference in your student's life with your encouragement.

Challenge:
- What are some ways you've recently encouraged your friends?
- Who is someone that needs encouragement?
- How might you encourage a different person every day this week?

Affirm:
- You are an encouragement by your life.
- I see God in you and it encourages me.
- You have many friends, so you must be a good encourager.
- What is the best way you encourage others?

Prayer:
- Who can we pray for that needs encouragement this week?
- How can we ask God to help you become an even better encourager?
- If you could ask God to change someone's life through encouragement, who would it be? Let's pray for that person.

Scripture:
You must warn each other every day, while it is still "today," so that none of you will be deceived by sin and hardened against God (Hebrews 3:13).

[1]Therefore, since we are surrounded by such a huge crowd of witnesses to the life of faith, let us strip off every weight that slows us down, especially the sin that so easily trips us up. And let us run with endurance the race God has set before us. [2]We do this by keeping our eyes on Jesus, the champion who initiates and perfects our faith. Because of the joy awaiting him, he endured the cross, disregarding its shame. Now he is seated in the place of honor beside God's throne. [3]Think of all the hostility he endured from sinful people; then you won't become weary and give up (Hebrews 12:1-3).

FAMILY RELATIONSHIPS

We all know that the teenage years can create strains in even the healthiest family. Your student may be facing some tough times at home right now. This lesson could open the door to some deep conversation.

Challenge:
- What are some specific ways you can honor your parents this week?
- What do you like best about your brother/sister?
- What do you like best about your parents?
- How can you go above the norm with your parents this week?
- How can you serve your brother/sister this week?

Affirm:
- You can be a great brother/sister because…
- You can make your family better by…
- I see you being a great family member by…

Prayer:
- I pray that God will heal you and your family in this area…
- I pray you will find the strength to serve/honor your parents.
- God, let us be the kind of brothers/sisters/sons/daughters that you want us to be.

Scripture:

"Honor your father and mother. Then you will live a long, full life in the land the Lord your God is giving you" (Exodus 20:12).

A friend is always loyal, and a brother is born to help in time of need (Proverbs 17:17).

They kept demanding an answer, so he stood up again and said, "All right, but let the one who has never sinned throw the first stone!" (John 8:7).

But Jesus said, "No, go home to your family, and tell them everything the Lord has done for you and how merciful he has been" (Mark 5:19).

FRIENDSHIP

Everybody wants friends. This topic will allow you to learn how your mentee values friends and what type of friends he or she has. You will also be able to encourage your student to be a good friend in order to have good friends.

Challenge:
- Who is it hard to be friends with, and why?
- Who is it easy to be friends with, and why?
- Do you have anyone who considers you a friend but you don't share that feeling?
- Is there anyone you consider a friend who might not share that feeling?

Affirm:
- I have seen you being a friend in this way...
- I think you have great qualities of being a good friend. They are...
- I see you becoming a great friend to some who are friendless.

Prayer:
- What friends can we pray for today?
- Do you have any friends who don't know Jesus as Savior?

Scripture:
A friend is always loyal, and a brother is born to help in time of need (Proverbs 17:17).

There are "friends" who destroy each other, but a real friend sticks closer than a brother (Proverbs 18:24).

⁹Two people are better off than one, for they can help each other succeed. ¹⁰If one person falls, the other can reach out and help. But someone who falls alone is in real trouble. ¹¹Likewise, two people lying close together can keep each other warm. But how can one be warm alone? ¹²A person standing alone can be attacked and defeated, but two can stand back-to-back and conquer. Three are even better, for a triple-braided cord is not easily broken (Ecclesiastes 4:9-12).

IDENTITY

The teenage years are filled with all kinds of issues involving identity and self-esteem. Your student may have huge struggles in this area. It's important to discover (or rediscover) the biblical foundation for who we are in Christ.

Challenge:
- How do you find your "worth" as a person?
- God uniquely designed you; how are you living like it?
- How are you allowing God to use your life for him?

Affirm:
- I see you are unique in this way...
- You are special to me in this way...
- It is so good to see someone who isn't trying to be just like everyone else.

Prayer:
- I pray God will show you that you are special this week.
- How can I ask God to use you and your uniqueness this week?

Scripture:

13You made all the delicate, inner parts of my body and knit me together in my mother's womb. 14Thank you for making me so wonderfully complex! Your workmanship is marvelous—how well I know it. 15You watched me as I was being formed in utter seclusion, as I was woven together in the dark of the womb. 16You saw me before I was born. Every day of my life was recorded in your book. Every moment was laid out before a single day had passed. 17How precious are your thoughts about me, O God. They cannot be numbered! 18I can't even count them; they outnumber the grains of sand! And when I wake up, you are still with me! (Psalm 139:13-18).

11Now these are the gifts Christ gave to the church: the apostles, the prophets, the evangelists, and the pastors and teachers. 12Their responsibility is to equip God's people to do his work and build up the church, the body of Christ (Ephesians 4:11-12).

This means that anyone who belongs to Christ has become a new person. The old life is gone; a new life has begun! (2 Corinthians 5:17).

OPPOSITE SEX

Dealing with the opposite sex is one of the best yet toughest things teenagers will experience as they mature. This week's curriculum will be a great help to the teenagers as they deal with the opposite sex. It's important to encourage teenagers to have friendships with the opposite sex—not just dating relationships. Understanding the value of just being friends will give your mentee a head start on most other teenagers.

Challenge:
- I want to challenge you to look at the opposite sex as friends first!
- How do you interact with members of the opposite sex?
- How can you become a friend with a member of the opposite sex without pursuing a dating relationship?

Affirm:
- Being friends with the opposite sex can teach you so much.
- I know that you are a great friend to guys/girls and I know you can be a great friend to the opposite sex. Just be yourself.

Prayer:
- What bothers you the most about being friends with members of the opposite sex? Let's pray about that.
- Are there any friends that we can pray for? What about?
- Is there something going on with a friend of the opposite sex that causes you to be uncomfortable? Let's ask God to help you get through that.

Scripture:
And now, dear brothers and sisters, one final thing. Fix your thoughts on what is true, and honorable, and right, and pure, and lovely, and admirable. Think about things that are excellent and worthy of praise (Philippians 4:8).

Respect everyone, and love your Christian brothers and sisters. Fear God, and respect the king (1 Peter 2:17).

³Let there be no sexual immorality, impurity, or greed among you. Such sins have no place among God's people. ⁴Obscene stories, foolish talk, and coarse jokes—these are not for you. Instead, let there be thankfulness to God (Ephesians 5:3-4).

OTHERS FIRST

This week you will invest in the life of your mentee by talking about Jesus' plan to put others first. This isn't a natural lifestyle for most of us—kids, teenagers, or adults! The main idea of this week is to allow your student to see that by putting others first, we bring joy to our own lives. Our hearts must be aligned with our actions. Just going through the motions will not make a deep difference in our lives.

Challenge:
- How do you put others first?
- Whom can you serve this week?
- How can you put your family first this week?
- What do you think it means to be a servant?
- How can you turn it up and be more of a servant?
- What does this saying mean: "I don't mind being a servant, as long as I'm not treated like one"?

Affirm:
- I see you being a servant in these ways…
- I think you are a servant-hearted person; here is how…
- I see you putting others first in this way…
- I know that your heart is focused on others because of…
- You are others-centered when I see you doing this…

Prayer:
- Who can we pray for that needs to be served this week?
- Is there someone who has served you, who we can thank God for?
- Who can I pray for that you need to put first?
- How can you put your friends first this week?
- How can you put your enemies first this week?

Scripture:
For you have been called to live in freedom, my brothers and sisters. But don't use your freedom to satisfy your sinful nature. Instead, use your freedom to serve one another in love (Galatians 5:13).

For you are free, yet you are God's slaves, so don't use your freedom as an excuse to do evil (1 Peter 2:16).

You see, we don't go around preaching about ourselves. We preach that Jesus Christ is Lord, and we ourselves are your servants for Jesus' sake (2 Corinthians 4:5).

⁵You must have the same attitude that Christ Jesus had. ⁶Though he was God, he did not think of equality with God as something to cling to. ⁷Instead, he gave up his divine privileges; he took the humble position of a slave and was born as a human being (Philippians 2:5-7).

STRUGGLES/ADVERSITY

Everyone goes through struggles but most people are caught off-guard when those moments arrive. This session will help your mentee prepare for dealing with the inevitable. Your student might not be facing any problems right now, but it's important to remember that those struggles will come. Helping your mentee prepare now could make a difference down the road.

Challenge:
- What is one lesson you've learned from a recent struggle?
- What is the hardest lesson you've learned from a struggle you have experienced?
- Do you know someone who is struggling right now that you can help through the rough time?

Affirm:
- I have seen how you handle problems in your life and you do such a good job.
- Thank you for being a good example to others by how you handle adversity.
- I believe you will be able to endure anything because you trust God so much.

Prayer:
- Are any of your friends having struggles that we can pray for?
- Are you going through any struggles that I could pray for?
- Do you see any struggles that you might encounter in the future we could pray for?

Scripture:
5Trust in the Lord with all your heart; do not depend on your own understanding. 6Seek his will in all you do, and he will show you which path to take (Proverbs 3:5-6).

2Dear brothers and sisters, when troubles come your way, consider it an opportunity for great joy. 3For you know that when your faith is tested, your endurance has a chance to grow. 4So let it grow, for when your endurance is fully developed, you will be perfect and complete, needing nothing (James 1:2-4).

In my distress I prayed to the Lord, and the Lord answered me and set me free (Psalm 118:5).

WISE CHOICES

Want to make a lifelong difference in the life of a teenager? Help your student understand the importance of making wise choices. We all face countless choices every day; making wise choices can make life extraordinary. Encouraging teenagers to think about the choices they make is an important first step.

Challenge:
- When do you find it most difficult to make good choices that go against what your friends want you to do?
- What are you doing now that you know you should stop doing because it's not godly? How can you change this pattern?
- How might your life be different if you started asking questions like "How is this good?" instead of "What's wrong with it?"
- What places cause you to make unwise choices, and why?
- What people do you hang around that make it easier for you to make unwise decisions?

Affirm:
- I see you standing up and making some hard choices like…
- You are strong in your beliefs; I see it here…
- You know godly things to do, and I see you doing it this way…

Prayer:
- What decisions are you facing that I could pray with you about?
- Is there anyone among your circle of friends who is making unwise choices and needs prayer?

Scripture:
I pray that your love will overflow more and more, and that you will keep on growing in knowledge and understanding (Philippians 1:9).

Teach me your decrees, O Lord; I will keep them to the end (Psalm 119:33).

If you need wisdom, ask our generous God, and he will give it to you. He will not rebuke you for asking (James 1:5).

YOU ARE GIFTED

Teenagers need to understand clearly that God created and uniquely gifted them. You as the mentor get a chance to really impact the life of your student this week by pointing out possible spiritual gifts and abilities. Help your student see that every Christian has spiritual gifts and natural talents, and God is ready to see those gifts and talents in action!

Challenge:
- What are some of your gifts and talents, and how are you using them?
- What are new ways you could use your gifts?
- How do your spiritual gifts benefit the body of Christ?

Affirm:
- I see you using your gifts in these ways...
- I know the Bible talks about everyone having gifts, and I think these might be some of yours...
- I am so glad that God gifted you in these ways...

Prayer:
- How can we ask God to use you and your gifts and talents?
- What are some things we can pray about possible uses for your gifts?
- Who can you bless this week by using your gifts?

Scripture:
Whatever is good and perfect comes down to us from God our Father, who created all the lights in the heavens. He never changes or casts a shifting shadow (James 1:17).

God has given each of you a gift from his great variety of spiritual gifts. Use them well to serve one another (1 Peter 4:10).

[6]In his grace, God has given us different gifts for doing certain things well. So if God has given you the ability to prophesy, speak out with as much faith as God has given you. [7]If your gift is serving others, serve them well. If you are a teacher, teach well. [8]If your gift is to encourage others, be encouraging. If it is giving, give generously. If God has given you leadership ability, take the responsibility seriously. And if you have a gift for showing kindness to others, do it gladly.

9Don't just pretend to love others. Really love them. Hate what is wrong. Hold tightly to what is good. 10Love each other with genuine affection, and take delight in honoring each other (Romans 12:6-10).

And the same is true for you. Since you are so eager to have the special abilities the Spirit gives, seek those that will strengthen the whole church (1 Corinthians 14:12).

MENTOR APPLICATION

Thank you for taking the time to complete this form. We want you to know that the following information will be kept confidential and will only be shared with appropriate ministry leaders.

Once you have completed the application, please return it to <u><<contact name here>></u> at <u><<email address here>></u> or by mail (<u><<physical address here>></u>).

Contact Information

Full Name: _____ Date: _____

Name You Prefer: _____ Gender: M ____ F ____

Email: _____

Address, City, ZIP: _____

Date of Birth: _____

Primary Phone: _____ Secondary Phone: _____

General Information

Occupation: _____ Employer: _____

Work Status: part time _____ full time _____ student _____ retired _____

Marital Status: single _____ married _____ divorced _____

Spouse's Name: _____

Children (and ages): _____

_____

Education

High School: _____ Year Graduated: _____

College / Trade School: _____ Year Graduated: _____

Degree: _____

Other Education: _____

References

Please list 2 people who are not relatives that you have known for more than 2 years. Please notify them that they will be contacted by a member of the mentor program leadership.

Name: _____

Primary Phone: _____

Email Address: _____

Relationship: _____

How long have you known this person and in what capacity? _____

_____

Name: _____

Primary Phone: _____

Email Address: _____

Relationship: _____

How long have you known this person and in what capacity? _____

_____

Personal Information

Write a brief testimony about how and when you trusted Jesus with your life.

Do you consider yourself to be a committed follower of Jesus?

How would you describe your current spiritual condition?

What kind of accountability do you have in your life (small group, mentor, and so on)?

What people or experiences have been most significant in your growth as a Christian?

Are there any issues or concerns that would have a negative impact on your commitment and involvement as a mentor? If so, please explain.

Are you able to make a one-year commitment to mentor a student?

Ministry Information

Please describe any past or present ministry or church experience.

List the dates and activities of other ministry experiences at this church, the leader of the ministry, and, if not current, reasons for ending your service.

Why do you want to be a mentor?

Do you have previous experience working with teenagers? If so, please explain.

Church Information

How long have you been attending this church? _____

Are you a member? _____

Please list any church training or spiritual development classes you have completed:

Please bring a copy of your driver's license and proof of car insurance to your interview.

LIFESTYLE AND LEGAL CONCERNS

In caring for teenagers, we believe it is our responsibility to seek adult mentors who can provide healthy, safe, and nurturing relationships. Please answer the following questions. Use an additional sheet of paper if necessary.

Are you currently part of a recovery group? If so, please give details.

Are you undergoing any treatment for depression or mental illness? If so, please give details.

Are you currently using or have you ever used illegal drugs? Yes _____ No _____

Have you ever gone through treatment for alcohol or drug abuse? Yes _____ No _____
If yes, please describe:

Have you ever been arrested and/or convicted of a crime? Yes _____ No _____
If yes, please describe:

Have you ever had sexual relations with a minor after you became an adult? Yes _____ No _____

Have you ever been accused or convicted of any form of child abuse? Yes _____ No _____
If yes, please describe:

Have you ever been a victim of any form of child abuse? Yes _____ No _____

If yes, would you like to speak to a counselor or pastor? Yes _____ No _____

Do you view X-rated movies, visit adult bookstores or clubs, read X-rated magazines, or look at Internet pornography? Yes _____ No _____

Are you willing to undergo a background check? Yes _____ No _____

If dating, are you pursuing a relationship that is honoring to God? Yes _____ No _____

Do you currently maintain a personal blog, website, MySpace, or Facebook account?
Yes _____ No _____
If yes, please provide the URL:

Do you have anything posted on your personal Internet site that would create a negative perception of our mentor ministry? Yes _____ No _____

I declare that the foregoing is true and correct. Ministry leaders may contact my references and appropriate government agencies to determine my suitability as a mentor. I understand that all this information will remain confidential.

Signature: _____ Date: _____

WHAT'S YOUR S.H.A.P.E.?

All Christians have a unique S.H.A.P.E.—spiritual gifts, heart or passion, abilities, personality, and experiences—that can be used to minister to others. By sharing your S.H.A.P.E., it will assist us in matching you with a mentee. Please return this completed form with your application.

What do you believe are your spiritual gifts?

1. _____

2. _____

3. _____

In what areas have you been able to use these gifts in the past?

What are three things you love to do?

1. _____

2. _____

3. _____

My strongest abilities are:
[A few examples might include drama, writing, speaking, fine arts, photography, video, counseling, computers, music, tutoring, athletics, and so on.]

1. _____

2. _____

3. _____

This is how I see myself:
[Circle the answer that best completes the sentence for you]

Around others, I am more...	**RESERVED**	**OUTGOING**
My decisions are based more on...	**FACTS/THINKING**	**FEELINGS**
In my relationships, I tend to be more...	**DEPENDENT on OTHERS**	**INDEPENDENT**
My use of time is more...	**DETERMINED**	**SPONTANEOUS**

When I have free time, I spend it:

What are some life experiences you feel might help you minister to a young person?

_____

_____

_____

WHAT WE BELIEVE

An important part of serving in the Mentoring Ministry is that you understand and commit to our doctrinal beliefs (taken from Saddleback Church). Please initial that you agree with the points below.

_____ **ABOUT GOD** God is the Creator and Ruler of the universe. He has eternally existed in three persons: the Father, the Son, and the Holy Spirit. These three are co-equal and are one God. Genesis 1:1,26,27; 3:22; Psalm 90:2; Matthew 28:19; 1 Peter 1:2; 2 Corinthians 13:14

_____ **ABOUT HUMANITY** Humanity is made in the spiritual image of God, to be like him in character. Humanity is the supreme object of God's creation. Although we have tremendous potential for good, we are marred by an attitude of disobedience toward God called "sin." This attitude separates humanity from God. Genesis 1:27; Psalm 8:3-6; Isaiah 53:6a; Romans 3:23; Isaiah 59:1,2

_____ **ABOUT ETERNITY** Humanity was created to exist forever. We will either exist eternally separated from God by sin, or in union with God through forgiveness and salvation. To be eternally separated from God is hell. To be eternally in union with him is eternal life. Heaven and hell are places of eternal existence. John 3:16; John 2:25; John 5:11-13; Romans 6:23; Revelation 20:15; 1 John 5:11-12; Matthew 25:31-46

_____ **ABOUT JESUS CHRIST** Jesus Christ is the Son of God. He is co-equal with the Father. Jesus lived a sinless human life and offered himself as the perfect sacrifice for the sins of all humanity by dying on a cross. He arose from the dead after three days to demonstrate his power over sin and death. He ascended to heaven's glory and will return again to earth to reign as King of kings, and Lord of lords. Matthew 1:22,23; Isaiah 9:6; John 1:1-5, 14:10-30; Hebrews 4:14,15; 1 Corinthians 15:3,4; Romans 1:3,4; Acts 1:9-11; 1 Timothy 6:14,15; Titus 2:13

_____ **ABOUT SALVATION** Salvation is a gift from God to humanity. We can never make up for our sin by self-improvement or good works. Only by trusting in Jesus Christ as God's offer of forgiveness can we be saved from sin's penalty. Eternal life begins the moment one receives Jesus Christ into his life by faith. Romans 6:23; Ephesians 2:8,9; John 14:6, 1:12; Titus 3:5; Galatians 3:26; Romans 5:1

_____ **ABOUT ETERNAL SECURITY** Because God gives humanity eternal life through Jesus Christ, the believer is secure in salvation for eternity. Salvation is maintained by the grace and power of God, not by the self-effort of the Christian. It is the grace and keeping power of God that gives this security. John 10:29; 2 Timothy 1:12; Hebrews 7:25; 10:10,14; 1 Peter 1:3-5

_____ **ABOUT THE HOLY SPIRIT** The Holy Spirit is equal with the Father and the Son as God. He is present in the world to make people aware of their need for Jesus Christ. He also lives in every Christian from the moment of salvation. He provides the Christian with power for living, understanding of spiritual truth, and guidance in doing what is right. The Christian seeks to live under his control daily. 2 Corinthians 3:17; John 16:7-13, 14:16,17; Acts 1:8; 1 Corinthians 2:12, 3:16; Ephesians 1:13; Galatians 5:25; Ephesians 5:1

_____ **ABOUT THE BIBLE** The Bible is God's Word to all humanity. It was written by human authors, under the supernatural guidance of the Holy Spirit. It is the supreme source of truth for Christian beliefs and living. Because it is inspired by God, it is truth without any mixture of error. 2 Timothy 3:16; 2 Peter 1:20,21; 2 Timothy 1:13; Psalm 119:105,160, 12:6; Proverbs 30:5

MENTOR INTERVIEW
WITH GUIDELINES

Things to think about when interviewing: Do you sense a humble, teachable spirit? Did the applicant connect with you in conversation? Did this person seem more interested in preaching at students or loving students? You don't need to lead the interview. Don't talk too much. Silence is OK!

Tell me about yourself. How would you describe yourself?

How did you become a Christian?

Tell me about your spiritual journey. Is there a person, thing, or event that has impacted your spiritual life more than any other?

What kind of accountability do you have in your life?

Are there any special issues happening in your life that would have an impact on your mentoring?

Go over the section of the application that addresses drinking, drugs, and lifestyle. Remind the applicant that he or she probably lives in the same community as the student who will be mentored.

Find out if the applicant has completed any required church training or spiritual development classes. We require that volunteers be church members before they start.

Describe any previous youth ministry experiences. What did you enjoy most about working with students?

Why do you want to be a mentor? **Hopefully, not to get their needs met. Also, we can't "fix" students. God is the one who changes and transforms lives.**

What would make you an asset to our mentor program? What are your strengths and weaknesses? **Look for specifics. Can this person be real and transparent?**

What do you think is more important in a mentor relationship: "following the rules" or building a relationship? Why? **We're looking for someone who is relational and flexible, not rigid.**

If you had an opportunity to attend some school, social, or church event that your student was participating in (such as sports game, music recital, school play, and so on), would you attend?

Do you have any hobbies or interests you would want to share with a student?

Do you have any ideas of what type of student you are interested in mentoring? **Need to let them know that we will do our best to prayerfully match them, but they should be open-minded. God may have something else in mind.**

Do you have any hesitations or fears about getting involved in this program? **Some fear is good; depend on God to guide the relationship.**

What, if any, are your expectations of the ministry and staff? **Explain that you will be available to help them work through any difficulties they face.**

Situational Questions

The following questions are based on different scenarios the mentor could be confronted with. We want to be sure that they are prepared for these situations that could arise:

Your student calls you on the phone and says that you have hurt his/her feelings. How do you respond?

You are a single mentor and a student asks you about your current sexual activity and reveals that he/she is sexually active. What should you say/do? **Looking for gut reaction. Does the applicant have good boundaries?**

You and your student are going to the movies and your student says, "I can see that R-rated movie. My parents let me see them all the time." How do you respond?

A student shares information that he/she is smoking pot and ditching school, and then says "Don't tell my parents." How should you handle this information? What if you can't contact me or someone else on the mentoring leadership team for a couple of days? What is your gut instinct? **You're wanting to see if the applicant knows to talk specifics. Why is the student doing this? Get details. Go together with student to talk to parents.**

A student shares that a family member has been molesting him/her, but asks you not to say anything to anyone because he/she is ashamed. He/she says, "If you tell someone, I will never trust you again." How do you respond? **Look for inappropriate shock reaction. Mentors need to be with these students in their pain and handle real situations. If they can't handle the interview, then they most likely won't be able to handle working with teenagers. Also, being a mentor is not about being liked by the student. They can't be afraid of losing the friendship.**

A student reveals that he/she has been feeling suicidal. What do you do with this information? **Find out if the student has a specific plan on how they will do it and when. Report this to mentor coach and get advice on telling parents, and so on.**

A student has run away from home and shows up on your doorstep. He/she says, "Don't tell my parents where I am." What do you do? **It's not OK to take the student in; it's against the law to harbor a runaway. Try to at least get the student to call parents to let them know where he/she is. If it's an abuse situation, call police—don't send them back home.**

Explain to the applicant that he/she will need to be fingerprinted, and provide the information on how to go about it. Explain the one-year commitment to the mentoring program. Ask if he/she needs to pray about it and discuss it with family before committing. Give the applicant the Mentor Commitment Form to fill out and give to you if you are ready, or take it home and mail back after prayerful consideration.

MENTOR COMMITMENT

After praying and talking with my family about the commitment involved with mentoring a young person, I choose to commit to the following:

I acknowledge the Lordship of Jesus Christ in my life, and I have a personal relationship with God through faith in Christ.

I am committed to growing and maturing in my relationship with God through devotional times, active attendance at church, and involvement in accountability. I am committed to stop serving if, at any time, my personal spirituality becomes compromised.

I am committed to a lifestyle that is both godly and above reproach. I commit to making wise choices. I realize that my lifestyle and decisions are a model for my mentee.

I am committed to attending the mandatory training and additional training throughout the year.

I will not post any pictures of my mentee on my personal blog, website, MySpace, or Facebook.

I will not post anything on my personal blog, website, MySpace, or Facebook that would be damaging to the reputation of the ministry or church.

I will commit to at least one year as a mentor to one student and will meet with my student weekly for at least an hour.

I commit to keeping matters confidential regarding my mentee and his or her family.

Name _____

Signature _____

Date _____

MENTOR REFERENCE FORM

_____ is applying to become a volunteer mentor with the youth ministry at _____ Church and has given your name as a personal reference.

Because mentors are in one-on-one relationships with students, we want to ensure that these relationships will be healthy ones. If you don't mind, we would like to ask you some questions. Your responses will remain confidential. You may use an additional sheet of paper if necessary.

Describe your relationship with this person.

How long have you known him/her?

How would you rate his/her ability in the following? You can give answers such as low, below average, average, very good, or excellent. And feel free to explain your answers:

- Involvement in peer relationships?

- Emotional maturity?

- Resolving conflict?

- Following through with commitments?

- Ability to relate to teenagers?

- Spiritual maturity?

What are his/her greatest strengths?

Do you have any concerns regarding him/her working with teenagers? Is so, please explain.

Thank you for your time.

_____   _____

Reference's Name   Date

_____

Reference's Signature

MENTOR COVENANT

Between

_____

and

_____

For one year, we commit ourselves to walk together in friendship as a unique expression of our mutual desire to become faithful followers of Jesus Christ. We promise to help, support, encourage, and pray for each other, and to the best of our abilities, we will participate in each other's lives in the following ways:

We will meet together on a regular basis.

    Frequency:

    Time:

    Place:

We will try to accomplish the following goals:

We will try to do some of the following activities together:

Signed: (mentor) _____

Signed: (student) _____

Date: _____

THE HOW-TO BOOKLET

Welcome to the mentor program! The goal of the mentor program is to put into action the last three goals of our ministry's purpose statement:

*"Our youth ministry exists to **REACH** non-believing students, to **CONNECT** them with other Christians, to help them **GROW** in their faith, and to challenge the growing to **DISCOVER** their ministry and **HONOR** God with their lives."*

Specifically, our mentoring program exists to support and challenge students, on a one-to-one basis and over time, to **GROW** in maturity and in their faith, to help them **DISCOVER** God's purpose and ministry for their lives, bringing **HONOR** to God.

With that said, let us give you the same charge that Paul gave to his apprentice, Timothy:

[2]Preach the word of God. Be prepared, whether the time is favorable or not. Patiently correct, rebuke, and encourage your people with good teaching... [6]As for me, my life has already been poured out as an offering to God. The time of my death is near. [7]I have fought the good fight, I have finished the race, and I have remained faithful. [8]And now the prize awaits me—the crown of righteousness, which the Lord, the righteous Judge, will give me on the day of his return. And the prize is not just for me but for all who eagerly look forward to his appearing (2 Timothy 4:2, 6-8).

BE ENCOURAGED! Together, and with God's help, we will have a tremendous year!

What You'll Find Inside

1. What We Want You to **Know**: Important Things to Keep in Mind

2. What We Hope You Will **Do**: Keys to Being a Mentor

3. Who We Hope You Will **Be**: Who You Are in Christ

WHAT WE WANT YOU TO KNOW
IMPORTANT THINGS TO KEEP IN MIND

What is the purpose?

The first purpose of our mentoring program is to help students **GROW** in their faith (or begin a relationship with Jesus Christ). We mentor to help students who may not be connected with a small group or our youth worship service, or who may need some extra support and encouragement.

The second purpose of our mentoring program is to help students realize that God has a purpose for their lives and that God has given them gifts to use for him **(DISCOVER)**.

The third purpose of our mentoring program is to help students get to the point where they strive to **HONOR** God with their lives.

Our students' stories vary greatly. Some come to us on their own accord for some extra support. Others are connected to us by their parents. Some of the students are from Christian families. Others are not. Parents/and or the students are in some way connected to our church when they begin the mentor relationship.

Understanding WHAT (grow, discover, honor) we're trying to do will help you be a more successful, more focused mentor.

Remember that you are not alone in this...

- God will give you wisdom and the tools necessary to help you mentor your student

- Your coaches are available for advice and prayer at all times

WHAT WE HOPE YOU WILL DO
(ADAPTED FROM ONE KID AT A TIME)

Be Consistent

Be dependable and trustworthy as a mentor. To the best of your ability, honor your commitments and keep your promises. Be there for the student you are mentoring on a regular and consistent basis for the length of time you committed to (one year from the time you start).

Be Yourself

Be thankful for who you are—for the personality, gifts, talents, abilities, and attributes that God has specifically given to you. Believe that God knows you, loves you, and has called you to serve as a mentor to youth. Be confident that God will be able to use you just the way you are.

Be a Listener

Take every opportunity to be a good listener in your mentoring relationship. Avoid judging and lecturing. Listen attentively because you care and because you desire to treat the student you are mentoring with dignity and respect.

Be Honest

Do your best to tell the truth always in your mentoring relationship, even when it hurts. In so doing, you will inspire the student you are mentoring to be honest with you. When either of you are unsure of the truth, be honest with each other and seek to discover the truth together.

Be Patient and Forgiving

Be realistic about the expectations you have for the student you are mentoring. Do your best to demonstrate unconditional love in every circumstance by being gracious, understanding, slow to anger, patient, and forgiving. Don't allow failures to destroy your relationship.

Be Encouraging

Bring out the best in the student you are mentoring by being generous with affirmation, encouragement, gratitude, and praise. Do all that you can to inspire your student to dream dreams and to recognize the potential that this teenager has in Christ Jesus.

Pray Hard

Don't become frustrated or discouraged because of your inability to change a young person's life. We can't "fix" students. That's the Holy Spirit's job. Instead, pray daily for the student you are mentoring, and trust God to do what you cannot do.

WE HOPE YOU WILL BE
WHO YOU ARE IN CHRIST

1. **Concerned about your spiritual health.**

   Be sure you are feeding yourself with God's Word and spending time with God. You should be healthy spiritually yourself to be able to minister to a young person. If at any time you feel that you cannot keep the commitments you made to the program or student, or if you are not in a good place spiritually, you should immediately let your coach or the coordinator know.

2. **The mentor God created you to be.**

   Explore the gifts God has given you. Take risks, and be ready for challenges. Don't compare yourself as a mentor or your student with other mentors or their students. Each relationship will be totally different and designed by God.

3. **A faithful person of prayer for your fellow mentors as well as your student.**

4. **Willing to be cared for.**

   Let your coaches care for you! Be ready to share about your ministry and share prayer requests.

THINGS YOU AND YOUR TEENAGER CAN DO TOGETHER

You can relax and just let your mentee be your guide. In this busy age, you can even just have your mentee over to help you clean your garage or run errands with you on occasion. You don't need to spend lots of money.

Since your one-on-one relationship will take time to build, try to avoid bringing someone else when you are with your mentee. However, you may include a third person (such as a friend or your spouse) from time to time or include your student on a family outing.

Try not to spend too much money on your mentee. Pricey entertainment shouldn't be the focal point of your relationship.

A few words of advice from a seasoned mentor: *"Adapt to your kid. If your kid wants to talk, bike, movie, catch, or whatever—do it, especially early on. It's the time, not the activity that counts."*

This list will help you offer some suggestions if your student isn't able to recommend an activity.

- Go to a sporting event (check local college and high school schedules as well as professional events)
- Go bike riding
- Help your mentee with his or her homework
- Go bowling
- Cook something together
- Go window-shopping
- Go miniature golfing
- Go out to eat or hang out at Starbucks
- Teach your mentee a craft
- Take a long walk
- Do a community service project together
- Go to the beach
- Go to the library or bookstore
- Have a picnic

- Talk about budgeting and credit cards
- Help your mentee prepare for a job interview
- Help your student look into colleges, including how to apply for financial aid
- Attend your mentee's school sport
- Do a Bible study
- Help your mentee learn how to set and achieve goals
- Go to a museum
- Take your mentee to your work
- Go on a mission trip together
- Shoot some hoops or hit some balls at a batting cage

HOW TO SHARE GOD
WITH YOUR TEENAGER

Be Real and Authentic
- Share your own spiritual struggles and/or challenges (without too many details).
- Share how God is working in your life currently or in the past.

Pray for Your Student
- Pray for God's timing and agenda.
- Pray that you will fully surrender to God's plan for your student (get yourself out of the way).
- Consistently pray for God's clear direction with the student.
- Ask your student how you can pray, and pray with your mentee if he or she is comfortable with you doing that.

Unconditionally Accept Your Student
- Focus on progress (even if it seems small). It's too easy to focus on the negative.
- Have realistic expectations of your student (remember where you were at that age).
- Help your student to feel valued and loved (not judged).
- Don't compare your student to other mentors' students.

Know Your Youth Ministry's Opportunities and Programs
- Talk with a staff member about helping your student get "plugged in."
- Be willing to attend various youth ministry functions with your student (examples: weekend worship services, summer camp, mission trip, and so on).
- Know the calendar of events for the youth ministry and encourage your student to participate.
- Work together with the youth ministry staff and volunteers who know your student.

Talk to Your Student About His/Her Relationship with God
- Ask your student questions (see "The Art of Asking Questions").
- Don't be afraid to be direct.

Share Your Favorite Verse or Bible Story Pertaining to Your Student's Needs
- Make sure your student has a Bible.
- Teach him/her how to look up verses.
- Teach your student how to apply Scripture to his/her life.

Know the "HABITS" (discipleship tools as found in *Purpose Driven Youth Ministry*) and Help Your Student Incorporate Them Into His/Her Life
- Understand the purpose of the "HABITS," and hold your student accountable to practicing them.

THE ART OF
ASKING QUESTIONS

Simply telling your mentee what he or she needs to know can be ineffective for at least two reasons:
- The student is passive and uninvolved.
- The student may not be convinced he or she needs the truth, and therefore the lesson won't make an impact.

The eternal truths of God and wisdom for everyday living are too important (and complex) to reduce to a lecture of platitudes and clichés. We need to master the art of asking questions.

A good question puts the ball in the court of the mentee. Questions create an opportunity for students to become more active participants. Good questions allow for self-discovery. Personal understanding and ownership can be facilitated by good questions. Teach young people to think for themselves!

Some Keys to Good Questions
- Discern the particular truth you hope to communicate, and then create good questions to lead your mentee there.
- Avoid yes-or-no questions. Go for questions that will cause your mentee to think deeper or share more details.
- Don't settle for the "right answer." When your mentee gives you a quick answer, is he saying something he believes, or just repeating something he's heard before? Ask your student, "OK, I hear what you're saying, but what does that really mean?"
- Be positive.
- Draw your mentee out by asking for more information. Ask questions like, "And then what did you do?" "How did you feel when that happened?" "How can I help you?"

The Art of Listening
Along with asking good questions you will need to be a good listener. There is a danger in wanting to supply a young person with answers too quickly. Teenagers want to be heard just as any of us do. Here are some tips for active listening:
- Offer your undivided attention. Don't try to listen when you are doing something else.
- Maintain eye contact.
- Accept what your student is saying. You don't have to agree, but give your mentee some encouragement by showing interest in what he or she is saying, and don't act like you are anxious to change the subject or offer your advice.

HELPING TEENAGERS AND FAMILIES IN CRISIS

It's important to be prepared for possible crisis situations. Having some procedures in place will give you confidence to handle those tough times. And it's important for you to know that you will not handle them alone; you will have your coach's or coordinator's guidance and support.

DO NOT ever tell a student you will keep a secret! Before allowing the student to proceed, tell her or him that you may not be able to do that depending on what she or he tells you. If it is something that is harmful to your mentee or another person, you will have to act on it. However, because you care so much for your mentee, you will be right there with her/him through the experience.

Contact your coach or coordinator immediately if any of the following situations arise. If the situation calls for a report to Child Protective Services (or the appropriate authorities for your area), the ideal action to take is to make the call with the student. But first, notify the coordinator or appropriate staff person to walk you through it.

DO what's right even though it is difficult. God can make something good come out of bad situations.

Here are some general guidelines for crisis situations:

Physical Abuse
If you suspect or are told about it:
- Don't overreact.
- Don't promise to keep the secret.
- Acknowledge the courage it took to tell someone.
- Get specific information—who the accused is, residence, date and time of incident or length of time abuse has occurred, and so on.
- Help the student notify parents if applicable and call Child Protective Services.

Drugs and Alcohol
- Talk with your mentee about the importance of wise choices.
- Love the student, not the behavior.
- Don't be afraid to confront your mentee or set boundaries.
- If this is a continuing problem, encourage your mentee to talk with his or her parents, and be there for that conversation. Talk about ways to help the student kick the habit.

Depression and Suicide

If the risk is moderate to high (the student has a plan to carry out a suicide attempt):

- Take immediate action. Don't leave your mentee alone. Release the student directly to informed parents or another relative. Again, go with your mentee to talk to either a parent or counselor.
- Trust your gut. If you suspect a student might be suicidal, ask!
- Listen with compassion. Get your mentee talking.
- Ask open-ended questions to assess the seriousness of the threat. Boil down the problem.
- Help your student establish coping strategies.
- Refer your mentee and family to a counselor (the church can help with this).

More commonly, there will be times when parents and a student clash and are having problems communicating. It is important for you not to get in the middle. Do not take sides or make judgments concerning any family conflict. However, sometimes getting caught in the middle is unavoidable and there may be opportunity for you to be a peacemaker. Discuss this with your coach or coordinator so a plan of action can be determined and they can be praying with you for God to work in this situation.

PARENT AFFIRMATION

I affirm this mentoring relationship and give (student) _____

permission to participate in the activities that will help build and strengthen this friendship.

In the event of illness or injury, I give (mentor) _____

permission to seek medical treatment as necessary should I not be reachable.

Signed: _____

Relationship to student: _____

Address: _____

Phone: (home) _____ (cell) _____

In case of emergency:

Other emergency contact: _____

Relationship to student: _____

Phone: (home) _____ (cell) _____

Doctor: _____ Phone: _____

Known allergies: _____

Date: _____

PARENT LETTER

Dear parents,

Thank you for giving us the opportunity to come alongside your teenager and be an encouragement to your child and your family. Our mentoring program exists to support students on a one-to-one basis as they **GROW** in maturity and in their faith, while helping them **DISCOVER** God's purpose for their lives as they move from adolescence to young adulthood. Mentors will "be there" for your teenager, offering encouragement and guidance, and being a role model.

Your approval and support of this mentoring relationship are critical. Therefore, we would like to answer some questions you may have. Here are some guidelines we hope you will find helpful:

It's OK for you to contact your child's mentor on occasion and keep lines of communication open. The mentor should give you his/her phone number, address, and any other information you need to stay in touch.

Communicate good things to the mentor. Many mentors go for weeks without getting any affirmation from their youth, so it's appreciated when parents give them a call and say, "Thanks for being there. You're doing a great job."

Inform the mentor of special concerns that you have. If you notice a particularly disturbing behavior in your child, believe your child is under an unusual amount of stress, or know your child is having difficult struggles with friends or a class at school, share this with the mentor so he or she will have a better understanding of what's going on. The mentor is not a family therapist, however, and should refrain from giving advice and counsel as if he or she is one.

Respect the mentor's right to keep information confidential. You need to know that it is possible your son or daughter will share things that mentors cannot share with you. This is not out of disrespect for you, but it allows the mentor to establish respect and trust with your teenager. You will need to trust the good judgment of the mentor on what to do with the information that he or she has been given. You need to respect the confidential nature of the mentoring relationship and not try to pump information out of the mentor concerning your child. If you trust the mentor, then there is a better chance that your teenager will trust him or her as well. The only information that a mentor is obligated to reveal to another person is information concerning evidence that your teenager may harm himself or herself or others.

Allow mentors to be themselves. They are not substitute parents. They may not approach things the same way you do. It will be helpful if you realize that your child's mentor is on your team, or, more correctly, on your family's team. A mentor has no intention of driving a wedge between you and your child. He or she will not take sides. The mentor's role is to be an authentic friend who will help your teenager to clarify his or her thinking on issues and make good decisions. Undoubtedly, the opinions or values of the mentor may be adopted, even if temporarily, by your teenager. This is normal. If you have a serious concern, you should discuss the situation with the mentor, youth ministry staff, or me.

Your teenager's mentor is trained and screened through our youth ministry. He or she will be carefully and prayerfully chosen for your teenager. We ask that the mentor and teenager spend a few times together to see if it is going to be a good match. If not, I will do my best to find another mentor for your child.

Please feel free to call me with any questions or concerns.

In his service,

APPLICATION LETTER

Dear _____,

I'm glad to know that you're interested in having a mentor. I've enclosed an application so I can get to know you better and be able to find a good match for you.

Please fill out the form and write anything else you think I should know on the back and return it to me. Right now, I don't have enough mentors for everyone so you may need to wait a couple months. While I am finding and training new mentors, consider trying a small group if you aren't in one already. There is a place on the application to check if you would like someone to contact you about getting started.

You may have questions about what a mentor is. This person is:
- Someone to talk to
- Someone to say, "You matter to me"
- Someone to challenge you to be your best
- Someone who takes you seriously
- Someone who doesn't judge you
- Someone who respects you
- Someone who accepts you
- Someone who understands you
- Someone to laugh with you
- Someone to be serious with you
- Someone who cares

If you decide to go forward with a mentor, you should know that it is a one-year commitment and you meet weekly for at least an hour with your mentor. You and your mentor will decide how you would like to spend the time.

Also, your parent(s) or guardian(s) will need to give permission for you to have a mentor. Once I have a mentor for you, I will call and talk to both you and your parent(s).

Thanks for taking this first step and get ready for God to bless you!

APPLICATION FOR A MENTOR

Name: _____ Date: _____

Address, City, ZIP: _____

Email:_____ Date of Birth: _____

Phone (home): _____ (cell): _____

Parent/Guardian Name(s): _____

School Attending: _____ Grade: _____

Do you attend our youth ministry worship services? □ Yes □ No □ Sometimes

Are you a Christian?   □ Yes, I'm sure   □ No   □ Not sure

Are you in a small group? □ Yes □ No
If so, which one? _____

If not, would you like to be contacted by someone from a local small group?
□ Yes □ No

What school or community activities do you participate in? _____

_____

What do you do for fun (hobbies, interests)? _____

_____

Please circle whichever words describe you:

Spiritual	Sensitive	Shy	Outgoing
Adventuresome	Talkative	Confident	Moody
Nervous	Friendly	Enthusiastic	Impatient
Impulsive	Serious	Bold	Analytical

Other: _____

Why are you interested in having a mentor? What would you like a mentor to help you with?

_____

_____

_____

MONTHLY MENTOR REPORT

Please complete this log by the last day of the month and return to your coach.

Mentor: _____

Mentee: _____

Coach: _____ Date: _____

Approximate total time spent this month on mentoring activities, including phone conversations and emails: _____

Summary of activities: _____

_____

_____

Do you feel like you are progressing in the mentor relationship? _____

_____

_____

Are you having any difficulties? Do you need any support? _____

_____

_____

Is there additional specific training or resources you would like to have? _____

_____

_____

Do you have any prayer requests for you/your student or praises to share? _____

_____

_____